Civil Service Qualifying (Non-Fast Stream) Test Guide

www.How2Become.com

As part of this product, you have also received FREE access to online tests that will help you to pass the Civil Service Tests.

To gain access, simply go to:

www.PsychometricTestsOnline.co.uk

Get more products for passing any test or interview at:

www.how2become.com

Orders: Please contact How2become Ltd, Suite 2, 50 Churchill Square Business Centre, Kings Hill, Kent ME19 4YU.

You can order through Amazon.co.uk under ISBN 9781910602089, via the website www.How2Become.com or through Gardners.com.

ISBN: 9781910602089

First published in 2015 by How2become Ltd.

Typeset for How2become Ltd by Anton Pshinka.

Disclaimer

Every effort has been made to ensure that the information contained within this guide is accurate at the time of publication. How2become Ltd are not responsible for anyone failing any part of any selection process as a result of the information contained within this guide. How2become Ltd and their authors cannot accept any responsibility for any errors or omissions within this guide, however caused. No responsibility for loss or damage occasioned by any person acting, or refraining from action, as a result of the material in this publication can be accepted by How2become Ltd.

The information within this guide does not represent the views of any third party service or organisation.

CONTENTS

INTRODUCTION TO
CIVIL SERVICE
TESTS

WHAT IS THE CIVIL SERVICE?

The UK Civil Service plays a significant role as part of the Government. The Civil Service helps to develop and implement new policies and procedures and enforce them in society. Foremost, they not only work alongside the Government, but they are the voices of society. They primarily provide a service directed to all the people across the country in order to support and assist issues such as:

- Paying benefits
- Healthcare
- Providing pension schemes
- Operating effective prison systems
- Issuing driving licenses and a range of other important development policies

People who work for the Civil Service are 'officials' who work under Government surveillance. They are co-ordinated and monitored by the Prime Minister to guarantee that policies are met and procedures are enforced. The Civil Service does not include all public sector employees. Employees of the Police Service, Armed Forces and Local Government and Councils are not part of the Civil Service.

The Civil Service are impartial and objective people in terms of political movements. The service that they provide does not reflect a certain political party. It merely demonstrates a non-political stance that is used to effectively maintain and enhance community procedures and policies. In other words, even if the leading Government and political party changes; this has no effect on the Civil Service. The Civil Service remains unaffected and serves the Government in power.

The Civil Service comes with great responsibility. Her Majesty's Civil Service was imposed to instigate and execute important decisions made by the Government, and thus it plays a vital role in all segments of society including safety, security and stability.

CIVIL SERVICE TESTS

This Civil Service Tests book will help you find your way to successfully pass the initial stages of the Civil Service recruitment process. Foremost, the purpose of this book is to ensure that you are fully prepared for the qualifying exams of the Civil Service.

This book will provide extensive information that will be relevant to your Civil Service tests. The book will also provide you with lots of questions to ensure that you are fully aware of what to expect and you understand how to answer the questions. We aim to give you a whole load of questions for you to work through in order to maximise your potential and successfully pass the testing stages to qualify as a civil servant.

The Civil Service play an accountable role in regards to both public and Government sectors. The Civil Service uses four key values to assess candidates:

- **Integrity** = the ability to put obligations of the public service above personal interests and/or beliefs.

- **Honesty** = being able to demonstrate high levels of truthfulness and openness.

- **Objectivity** = being able to display objective views and opinions on certain areas. Basing decisions and policies on rigorous analysis and evidence to form a plausible and valid outcome.

- **Impartiality** = being able to serve the power of the Government in charge and meet the needs and merits in which they enforce.

This book is a learning aid for anyone wishing to pursue a career in the Civil Service. Understanding the different stages of the selection process is important. Each question type is there for a reason. All of the questions in this book are questions that are often used in the Civil Service Tests, so it is imperative you know how to answer them!

THE AIMS AND OBJECTIVES OF THE BOOK

If you are about to take or contemplating about taking the Civil Service tests, you need to establish whether you are cut out for the role.

The aim of this book is simple. It gives clear and detailed information on everything you will need to know in terms of the selection process and the routes available into the Civil Service.

Objectives of this book are to provide:

* 100% preparation for the Civil Service Tests.
* Detailed explanations about each section of the tests, so you know what to expect.
* General tips for passing the different routes of the Civil Service Tests.
* Lots of questions for you to work through at your pace.
* A simple layout which is easy to follow.
* Different practice tests, depending on the route you are considering on taking into the Civil Service.

HOW TO WORK THROUGH THE BOOK

The book follows a simple structure. Depending on the role you are thinking of applying for in regards to the Civil Service, will depend on the route you will need to take. There are different routes that you can take:

* **Administrative Grade Tests**
* **Non-Fast Managerial Grade Tests**

Your test will depend on what job role you are applying for within the Civil Service. Therefore, it is important to know what test you will be sitting. However, all the tests in this book will ensure that you are fully prepared in any of the routes you wish to take.

The chapters in this book are based on one of the routes you can take into the Civil Service (**Administrative** and **Non-Fast Stream Managerial**). Each chapter starts off with a detailed explanation. You will then be given lots and lots of testing questions to work through.

At the end of each sub-chapter, you will be able to check your answers. Make sure you do check your answers because it is just as important to know where you went wrong, as it is getting the question right. Take the time to understand each question type thoroughly to ensure maximum potential, before moving on through the testing process.

STRUCTURE OF THE BOOK

The structure of the book is very simple. The first section of the book applies to candidates who are required to take the Administrative Grade Tests. The second half of the book focuses on the Managerial (Non-Fast Stream) Tests. Each test will be broken down into sub-sections to provide a carefully and thorough overview of what you can expect for each question. The structure of the book will follow this layout:

- **General Tips for Passing the Civil Service Tests**

- **Administrative Grade Tests**
    - o Handling Data
    - o Data Interpretation
    - o Quantitative Reasoning
    - o Correct Sentence
    - o Word Swap
    - o Missing Words
    - o Following Procedures
    - o Speed and Accuracy

- **Managerial Tests**
    - o Personality Tests
    - o Attitudinal Tests
    - o Situational Awareness Tests

Finally, we have also provided you with some additional free online psychometric tests which will help to further improve your competence in this particular testing area. To gain access, simply go to:

www.PsychometricTestsOnline.co.uk

Good luck and best wishes,

The How2become team

CHAPTER 1

GENERAL TIPS FOR PASSING CIVIL SERVICE TESTS

GENERAL TIPS FOR PASSING THE CIVIL SERVICE TESTS

- Practice makes perfect! Ensure that you are fully prepared by familiarising yourself with the test.

- Be prepared! It is important that you are prepared for your tests. Practicing for these tests will offer the best solution to ensure your success.

- Read everything carefully and ensure you understand what the questions are asking before answering them.

- Make sure you practice your mathematical skills. You will find the numerical reasoning test difficult if you are not great at maths. Practice your adding, subtracting, multiplying and dividing. Also practice other mathematical skills including fractions, percentages and ratios.

- The situational awareness test requires a considerable amount of attention to detail. Pay attention and read through everything carefully. Do not skim through the information as you may miss something that could be vital in choosing the correct answer.

- The practice tests should be worked through with little distraction. You want to fully concentrate on these tests, which in turn will make you feel more positive when it comes to taking your real test.

- The personality and attitude tests do not have wrong or right answers. However, they could impact your application. Although you want to answer them truthfully, you need to remember that your application will be assessed on your answers regarding your behaviour, personality and attitude towards social situations.

- Remember, these tests are here to assess your abilities and knowledge and ascertain whether you are a valuable candidate in regards to the Civil Service.

- Lack of self-esteem and preparation will make you feel more apprehensive and anxious which may affect your ability to perform in these tests. They could affect your marks and so you need to ensure that you are fully prepared and knowledgeable of the tests. By doing this, you will feel less pressure, have more confidence, and you are more likely to succeed in the real test.

- Stay calm, stay focused and stay positive!

CHAPTER 2

ADMINISTRATIVE GRADE TESTS

As you would expect, the term "administrative" in the Civil Service, is just like any other administrative role. If you join the Civil Service as an administrator, you will be involved in: clerical, numerical and verbal duties including operating computer systems, filing, updating records, interacting with customers, financial administration and dealing with queries, complaints and other important information.

Administrative roles have great responsibility. They are in charge of making sure important documentation, reports, records and data are kept up to date, organised and managed proficiently.

The **Administrative Grade Tests** are used to assess a candidate's capabilities and skills in regards to administrative roles, in hope to determine whether a candidate is qualified and suitable for the job role.

Such tests are designed to help the recruitment process. The recruitment process is a key stage for all the people involved. Not only is it the first step for someone to qualify as a member of the Civil Service, but the Civil Service need to ensure they choose compliant, effective and responsible workers.

The Civil Service use these tests as a way to explore psychometrics. They are designed to measure a person's level of skills, knowledge, ability, attitude and performance to decide whether or not someone is rightly suitable for the job role.

WHAT TO EXPECT ON THE DAY

On the day of your test, you will be invited to attend a test centre. Your test will either be pen-to-paper or computer based; either way it will not make a difference to the test itself. Take comfort in the fact that you will not be alone. In fact, there will be several others there that day taking the same test you are, so try to stay relaxed and focused. A test administrator will then begin to explain the rules and regulations of sitting the test (this will take you back to your school days when you had to sit and wait for the invigilator to start the test). You will be told all the information about the test, your time limit for example, and then your test will begin.

Note: If you suffer with a disability or have a learning disability, please notify the department or agency prior to sitting the test. You will not be penalised, if anything, this will help you. Whether you need extra time, or need someone to read the questions etc. You won't receive this benefit if you do not notify them prior to the day of your test.

STRUCTURE OF THE TEST

The following questions in this chapter will indicate the types of questions you will face in the Administrative Grade Tests. It is important to work carefully through each question type and understand how to answer the questions.

Please note that whilst this chapter indicates all the question types that you could be faced with, depending on the test you are sitting will depend on how relevant each question type is. So, be sure to know what test you will be sitting and practice those questions intensively. Although, practicing all the question types will not hurt, in fact the more question types you get to grips with, the more prepared you will feel and the more chance you have at passing the test.

The administrative grade chapters will be broken down into sub-sections, each dealing with a particular question type:

- **Handling Data**
- **Data Interpretation**
- **Quantitative Reasoning**
- **Correct Sentences**
- **Word Swap**
- **Missing Words**
- **Following Procedures**
- **Speed and Accuracy**

For some of the Civil Service Tests, you are permitted to use a calculator. However, for the purpose of practicing, we advise that you do not use a calculator. This will ensure that you are knowledgeable and have revised fully in terms of mental arithmetic. You will feel much more comfortable and prepared knowing you can answer at least some of the questions without a calculator.

By all means, use a calculator if you are really stuck or to check your answers after completion to ensure you know how to get to the correct answer.

We have also not provided you with a time limit. This will allow you to work slowly and carefully through the chapters. Read each question thoroughly and answer the question accordingly.

GENERAL TIPS FOR PASSING THE ADMINISTRATIVE GRADE TESTS

- Ensure your mathematical skills are up to scratch. People who struggle with maths may find this test somewhat difficult. A lot of the questions are based on mathematics. Therefore you need to fully grasp how to answer the questions.

- Try and practice these questions without a calculator. This will make you feel more confident when it comes to your real test.

- Make sure you check your answers to these practice questions in order to learn from your mistakes. Understanding where you went wrong will help you significantly when you take another test.

- Educated guesses are worthwhile. If you find yourself stuck on a question that offers multiple choice, you should answer it anyway. You are probably able to eliminate some of the obscure answers and then take an educated guess. This way you are more likely to gain a couple of extra marks here and there, as opposed to not answering them at all.

CHAPTER 3

(HANDLING DATA)

ADMINISTRATIVE GRADE TESTS

Handling data; it is pretty much exactly what it says! You will be given numerical data and you will have to answer the question accordingly. You should be able to answer these questions without a calculator in the time frame of approximately 30 seconds per question. So it is important that you practice! Practice makes perfect; you will begin to see yourself improving and see that you are becoming quicker and more accurate at answering the questions.

We have deliberately provided you without a time frame in order for you to work through the questions carefully. You need to understand how the section works and how to get to the right answer. If you don't reach the right answer, you need to take the time to figure out where you went wrong. You have 60 questions to answer in this section.

EXAMPLE

Question

A medium-sized egg weighs 60 grams. What would be the weight if you had 9 medium-sized eggs?

How to work it out

- 1 medium-sized egg weighs 60 grams.
- You want to work out the weight of 9 medium-sized eggs.
    60 multiplied by 9 = 540

Answer

540 grams

Question 1

A bakery sells a croissant for £1.20. How much will it cost to buy 11 croissants?

Answer

Question 2

Sam raised £560 for charity by giving music lessons. Sam charges £8.00 per lesson. How many lessons did Sam give?

Answer

Question 3

Three people went to the supermarket. They split the cost between them. The total comes to £213.75. How much will each person have to pay?

Answer

Question 4

Robert was sponsored £1.25 for every mile he ran. Robert managed to raise £11.25. How many miles did Robert run?

Answer

Question 5

Millie goes to the pet store. She buys 2 cats, 5 goldfish and 3 guinea pigs. A cat costs £14.30, a goldfish costs 70p and a guinea pig costs £11.60. In total, how much does Millie spend?

Answer

Question 6

Eggs are sold in boxes of six or twelve. What is the lowest amount of boxes you could buy if you wanted to buy exactly 36 eggs?

Answer

Question 7

Three people are going on holiday. In total, the holiday would cost £2,281.50. On average, how much would it cost per person?

Answer

Question 8

Joe had 40 magic beans. He plants ¾ of them. How many magic beans does Joe have left?

Answer

Question 9

250 grams of coffee in one jar. How many jars would there be if there is 2000 grams of coffee?

Answer

Question 10

A gas bill gets charged 11.5p extra for every unit they go over. If someone goes over by 54 units, how much extra will they have to pay?

Answer

Question 11

January has 31 days. That month Ryan received £1742.51 by working every day. How much did Ryan earn each day?

Answer

Question 12

Elizabeth draws 13 squares. In total, how many degrees are there?

Answer [   ]

Question 13

A taxi costs £3.60 for every mile. If someone travels 7 miles, how much will they have to pay?

Answer [   ]

Question 14

What is 456 divided by 8?

Answer [   ]

Question 15

What is 42 multiplied by 11?

Answer [   ]

Question 16

A service charge of 15% is added to the bill at a restaurant. The meal came to £58.00. How much will their service charge be?

Answer [   ]

Question 17

Gareth spent £146.35 in one shop and £75.95 in another shop. How much money did Gareth spend altogether?

Answer

Question 18

An ambulance received a call at 1430 hours. It took them 45 minutes to reach the scene of the accident. What time did the ambulance arrive at the scene?

Answer

Question 19

A flight to France was leaving at 0230am. People arrived at the airport at 2345 hours. How long would they have to wait until the flight was leaving? (Assuming the flight was leaving on time).

Answer

Question 20

If a concert ticket costs £33.60 each and a group of 8 people go, how much in total would the group spend?

Answer

Question 21

A train is leaving at 1340 hours. The journey takes approximately 3 hours and 15 minutes. What time will the train arrive at the destination?

Answer

Question 22

A bus is scheduled to arrive every 15 minutes. How many buses (considering they were on time) could we expect in 3 hours and 45 minutes?

Answer [   ]

Question 23

The sterling to euro rate is 1:1.26. How many euros would you receive if you changed up £20?

Answer [   ]

Question 24

The sterling to US dollar rate is 1:1.60. How many dollars would you receive if you changed up £450?

Answer [   ]

Question 25

Linda is hiking. She gets out her compass. She is facing west. If she turns three right angles clockwise, what way will she be facing?

Answer [   ]

Question 26

A family of 4 split the cost of all the household bills equally. The water bill was £80.40, the gas bill was £35.00 and the electric bill was £40.00. The rent for the month was £490. How much does each member of the family put towards covering all the bill costs?

Answer

Question 27

What is 560 divided by 7?

Answer

Question 28

A kilogram of cheese costs £13.00. How much would it cost for 550 grams of cheese?

Answer

Question 29

A litre of milk costs £1.95. How much would it cost for 17 litres of milk?

Answer

Question 30

A flight leaves the airport at 2200 hours. It is an 11 hour and 45 minute flight. There is a 2 hour time difference. What is the time the flight arrives at it's destination, assuming the time difference is 2 hours in front?

Answer

Question 31

An exam is 2 hours and 30 minutes long. There are 3 sections. If you split your time equally, how long would you spend on each section?

Answer

Question 32

A woman goes into a shop to do her grocery shop. She gets a discount for having a store card. Her discount is 15%. The total comes to £195.00. How much does she have to pay if she uses her discount card?

Answer

Question 33

A wallet contains two £20 notes, four £5 notes, a fifty pence coin and a 20 pence coin. How much is in the wallet?

Answer

Question 34

Subtract 150 from 400, subtract 20 and multiply by 3. What number do you have?

Answer [ ]

Question 35

There are 24 hours in the day. How many hours are there in one week?

Answer [ ]

Question 36

A car journey usually takes 4 hours and 55 minutes. They get stuck in a traffic jam for 75 minutes. How long does this car journey take altogether?

Answer [ ]

Question 37

There are seven people in a team. Three of them weigh 70 kg each. The remaining four weigh 75 kg. What is the average weight of the team? Round up to 1 decimal place.

Answer [ ]

Question 38

A bathroom floor needs 48 tiles. A box contains 6 tiles. How many boxes will be needed to cover the bathroom floor?

Answer [ ]

Question 39

James went to sleep at 10:30pm. He got exactly 8 hours and 35 minutes sleep. What time did James wake up?

Answer

Question 40

You pay £63.30 per month for your council tax. How much would you have spent on council tax for three quarters of the year?

Answer

Question 41

You walk 15 miles. It takes you 3 hours. What speed are you walking at in miles per hour?

Answer

Question 42

The perimeter of a building site is 320 metres. The site has a square perimeter. What is the length of each side of the site?

Answer

Question 43

Mia left home and drove at the rate of 50 mph for 2 hours. She stopped for lunch at a restaurant. She drove for another 4 hours at 55 mph. How many miles did Mia drive?

Answer

Question 44

Liam biked at the rate of 15 mph for 5 hours. How many miles did Liam bike?

Answer

Question 45

Helen is going out to a nightclub. In her purse she has three £20 notes, one £10 note, three £5 notes and 4 pound coins. How much money does Helen have?

Answer

Question 46

Jessica goes shopping. She wants to buy a new dress for a wedding. The dress she likes is £75.00. She only has £60. However, the dress is on sale for 20%. How much will the dress cost her?

Answer

Question 47

What is 2/3 of 60?

Answer [   ]

Question 48

What is 35% of 120?

Answer [   ]

Question 49

A bus leaves at 11:15am. The bus journey is 2 hours and 38 minutes long. What time does the bus arrive at the destination?

Answer [   ]

Question 50

A cat has a litter of 4 kittens. Assuming each kitten has the same number of litter, how many cats would there be in total? (Including the original cat).

Answer [   ]

Question 51

There are 16 girls in a class. There are 20 boys. What is the ratio of girls to boys in the class? Write your answer in its simplest form.

Answer [   ]

Question 52

The perimeter of a playground is 1600 metres. Assuming the playground is square, what is the length of each side of the playground?

Answer

Question 53

A kitchen needs 88 flooring tiles. A box of tiles comes in packs of 5. How many boxes will be needed to make sure that they have enough tiles to complete the kitchen floor?

Answer

Question 54

A multi-storey car park has 6 floors and can hold 61 cars on each floor. Also, the car park has 5 allocated car parking spaces per floor for disabled people. How many spaces are there in the multi-storey car park?

Answer

Question 55

Peter spends 2 hours on the phone to his girlfriend who is abroad. If the call costs 15p every 5 minutes, how much does the call cost him?

Answer

Question 56

There are 60 seconds in 1 minute. How many seconds are there in 14 minutes?

Answer

Question 57

A service charge is added to the bill at the Christmas party work meal. The charge is 20%. The meal came to £348. What will be the total cost of the meal including the service charge?

Answer

Question 58

A square has an area of 121 cm2. What is the perimeter of the square?

Answer

Question 59

The length of a rectangle is 12cm. The width of the rectangle is 4.5cm. What is the area of the rectangle?

Answer

Question 60

What is the average between 131, 210 and 296? Round it up to the nearest whole number.

Answer

ANSWERS TO HANDLING DATA

Q1. £13.20

EXPLANATION = 1.20 x 11 = 13.20

Q2. 70

EXPLANATION = 560 / 8 = 70

Q3. £71.25

EXPLANATION = 213.75 / 3 = 71.25

Q4. 9

EXPLANATION = 11.25 / 1.25 = 9

Q5. £66.90

EXPLANATION = 2 cats = 28.60, 5 goldfish = £3.50, 3 guinea pigs = 34.80. So, 28.60 + 3.50 + 34.80 = 66.90

Q6. 3

EXPLANATION = 36 eggs, lowest number of boxes would be = 3 boxes of 12

Q7. £760.50

EXPLANATION = 2,281.50 / 3 = 760.50

Q8. 10

EXPLANATION = 40 / 4 = 10

Q9. 8

EXPLANATION = 2000 / 250 = 8

Q10. £6.21

EXPLANATION = 11.5 x 54 = 621p = £6.21

Q11. £56.21

EXPLANATION = 1742.51 / 31 = 56.21

Q12. 4680

EXPLANATION = 1 square = 90 x 4 = 360 degrees. 360 x 13 = 4680

Q13. £25.20

EXPLANATION = 3.60 x 7 = 25.20

Q14. 57

EXPLANATION = 456 / 8 = 57

Q15. 462

EXPLANATION = 42 x 11 = 462

Q16. £8.70

EXPLANATION = 58 /100 x 15 = 8.70

Q17. £222.30

EXPLANATION = 146.35 + 75.95 = 222.30

Q18. 1515 or 3.15 pm

EXPLANATION = 1430 = 2.30 pm + 45 minutes = 3.15 pm or 1515

Q19. 2 hours and 45 minutes

EXPLANATION = difference between 2345 and 0230 = 165 minutes = 2 hours and 45 minutes

Q20. £268.80

EXPLANATION = 33.60 x 8 = 268.80

Q21. 1655 or 4.55pm

EXPLANATION = 1.40 pm + 3 hours = 4.40pm + 15 minutes = 4.55pm or 1655

Q22. 15

EXPLANATION = 1 bus = 15 minutes. 3hrs and 45 minutes = 225 minutes / 15 = 15

Q23. 25.2 euros

EXPLANATION = £1 = 1.26 euros. £20 = 20 x 1.26 = 25.2

Q24. $720

EXPLANATION = £1 = 1.60 US dollars. £450 = 450 x 1.60 = 720

Q25. South

EXPLANATION = she is facing west, she turns three right angles clockwise. 1 turn = north, 2 turns = east, 3 turns = south.

Q26. £161.35

EXPLANATION = 80.4 + 35 + 40 + 490 = 645.40 = 645.40 / 4 = 161.35

Q27. 80
EXPLANATION = 560 / 7 = 80

Q28. £7.15
EXPLANATION = 1 kilogram = 1000 grams. So, 550g would equal 13.00 / 1000 x 550 = 7.15

Q29. £33.15
EXPLANATION = 1.95 x 17 = 33.15

Q30. 11.45am
EXPLANATION = 10pm + 11 hours 45 minutes = 09.45. Plus 2 hours time difference (ahead) = 11.45am

Q31. 50 minutes
EXPLANATION = 2 hours and 30 minutes = 150 minutes / 3 = 50

Q32. £165.75
EXPLANATION = 195 / 100 x 15 = 29.25. 195 - 29.25 = 165.75

Q33. £60.70
EXPLANATION = £20 + £20 + £4 x £5 = £20 + 50p + 20p = £60.70

Q34. 690
EXPLANATION = 400 -150 - 20 x 3 = 690

Q35. 168 hours
EXPLANATION = 24 (hours) x 7 (days) = 168

Q36. 6 hours and 10 minutes
EXPLANATION = 4 hours and 55 minutes + 75 minutes (1hr and 15mins) = 6 hours and 10 minutes

Q37. 72.9 kg
EXPLANATION = 70 x 3 = 210. 75 x 4 = 300. 210 add 300 = 510 / 7 = 72.85. To 1 decimal place = 72.9

Q38. 8 boxes
EXPLANATION = 48 / 6 = 8

Q39. 7:05 am

EXPLANATION = 10.30pm + 8 hours and 35 minutes = 7.05 am

Q40. £569.70

EXPLANATION = three quarters of the year = 9 months. 9 x 63.30 = 569.70

Q41. 5 mph

EXPLANATION = 15 (miles) / 3 (hours) = 5 mph

Q42. 80 metres

EXPLANATION = 320 / 4 = 80 metres

Q43. 320 miles

EXPLANATION = Distance = 50 x 2 = 100. 4 x 55 = 220. 220 + 100 = 320 miles

Q44. 75 miles

EXPLANATION = Distance = 15 x 5 = 75

Q45. £89

EXPLANATION = 20 + 20 + 20 +10 + 5 + 5 + 5 + 4 = 89

Q46. £60

EXPLANATION = 75 / 100 x 20 = 15. So, 75 - 15 = 60

Q47. 40

EXPLANATION = 60 / 3 x 2 = 40

Q48. 42

EXPLANATION = 120 / 100 x 35 = 42

Q49. 1353pm / 1.53pm

EXPLANATION = 11:15am add 2 hours and 38 minutes = 1353pm / 1.53pm

Q50. 21

EXPLANATION = 1 cat has 4 kittens = 5 cats in total. Each kitten has 4 kittens each = 16 new kittens. 16 + 5 = 21

Q51. 4:5

EXPLANATION = you need to find the biggest number that 16 and 20 can be divided by. They both can be divided by 4. 16 / 4 = 4. 20 / 4 = 5. So 4:5

Q52. 400 metres

EXPLANATION = 1600 / 4 = 400

Q53. 18 boxes

EXPLANATION = 88 tiles / 5 = 17.6. So, you would need another box to make sure you had enough. So 18 boxes would be needed.

Q54. 396

EXPLANATION = 61 x 6 = 366. 5 x 6 = 30. So, 366 + 30 = 396

Q55. £3.60

EXPLANATION = there are 12 x 5 minutes per hour. So, 12 x 15p = 1.80. For 2 hours = £3.60

Q56. 840 seconds

EXPLANATION = 60 x 14 = 840

Q57. £417.60

EXPLANATION = 348 / 100 x 20 = 69.60. 69.60 + 348 = 417.60

Q58. 44

EXPLANATION = the clue is the 'square'; each side will be the same size, if the area is 121, it means each side is 11cm (area = 11 x 11 = 121). So the perimeter would be 11 + 11 + 11 + 11 = 44.

Q59. 54cm2

EXPLANATION = 12 x 4.5 = 54

Q60. 212

EXPLANATION = 131 + 210 + 296 = 637. 637 / 3 = 212.333. To the nearest whole number = 212

Now move on to the next section of the guide.

CHAPTER 4

(DATA INTERPRETATION)

ADMINISTRATIVE GRADE TESTS

Data interpretation is used as a way to assess a candidate's ability to extract information from tables, charts and graphs then answer the questions that follow in relation to that data. The data extracted has to be analysed and manipulated to find the correct answer. For each graph, chart or table you are presented with, 5 questions will follow. There are 35 questions to answer in total. Carefully read each question carefully and then analyse the data to work out the answer.

Please circle the correct answer.

EXAMPLE

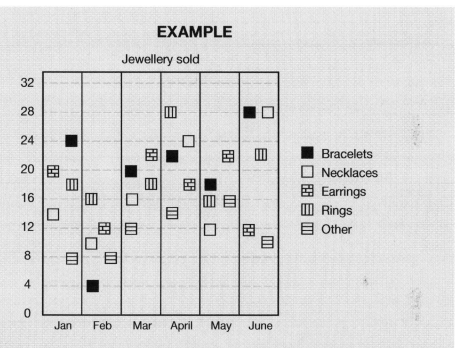

Question
How many bracelets were sold over the 6 month period?

How to work it out
- Bracelets =   January = 24 February = 4 March = 20 April = 22 May = 18 June = 28
- 24 + 4 + 20 + 22 + 18 + 28 = 116

Answer
116

*Based on 100 students and their marks in English,
Maths and Science examinations.*

Marks out of 40				
Subject	30 and above	20 and above	10 and above	0 and above
English	19	52	91	100
Maths	13	36	90	100
Science	11	42	87	100
AVERAGE	11	43	89	100

Question 1. If at least 50% in their examination is needed to go on to higher education, how many students in Maths can go on to higher education?

A	B	C	D	E
49	13	36	19	27

Question 2. What is the percentage of students who achieved marks 20 or above in their English exam?

A	B	C	D	E
36%	41%	56%	52%	48%

Question 3. What is the difference between the number of students who achieved 30 or above in English, and the number of students who achieved 20 and above in Science?

A	B	C	D	E
23	25	27	31	19

Question 4. The number of students scoring less than 50% marks, in terms of average, is?

A	B	C	D	E
43	57	21	17	53

Question 5. What subject had the highest number of students who scored below 10?

A	B	C	D	E
English	Maths	Science	All the same	English and Maths

Production of computer software (in thousands) between 1995 and 2002

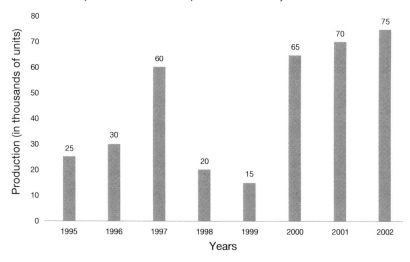

Question 6. What is the average number of computer software produced between 1995 and 2002?

A	B	C	D	E
61,000	36,000	21,000	45,000	52,000

Question 7. What was the decline in percentage in the production of computer software from 1997 to 1998? To the nearest whole number.

A	B	C	D	E
33%	41%	67%	69%	53%

Question 8. What was the percentage increase in the production from 1999 to 2000?

A	B	C	D	E
219%	183%	271%	333%	312%

Question 9. What year saw the biggest decrease in production from the previous year?

A	B	C	D	E
1995	1998	1999	2001	2002

Question 10. What is the difference between the lowest and the highest production years?

A	B	C	D	E
60,000	35,000	65,000	70,000	85,000

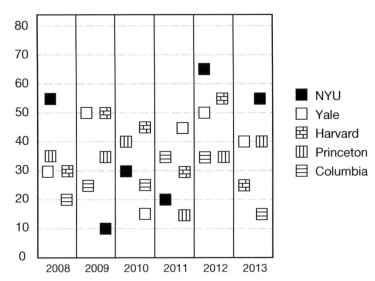

Medical Papers Published

Question 11. In what year did NYU publish the most medical papers?

A	B	C	D	E
2008	2011	2010	2012	2009

Question 12. How many medical papers were published by Yale in 2009?

A	B	C	D	E
35	25	50	40	75

Question 13. In total, how many papers did Princeton publish from 2008 to 2013?

A	B	C	D	E
185	200	105	210	225

Question 14. In what year did Columbia and Princeton publish the same number of papers?

A	B	C	D	E
2011	2010	2009	2008	2012

Question 15. How many papers were published in 2011?

A	B	C	D	E
125	145	110	95	205

Employees in departments of a company

Department	January	February	March	April	May	June
Marketing	21	24	17	15	23	27
Admin	18	11	15	13	13	18
Sales	21	22	29	31	28	24
IT	19	13	17	18	22	25

Question 16. How many employees are there in May?

A	B	C	D	E
71	78	83	86	89

Question 17. What was the average number of employees for February?

A	B	C	D	E
9.75	17.5	11.5	13	19.75

Question 18. What was the average number of Admin employees over the 6 month period? To the nearest whole number.

A	B	C	D	E
11	17	15	21	24

Question 19. What was the largest number of people employed at one given time? (I.e. in any month, in any department).

A	B	C	D	E
29	31	27	35	26

Question 20. What is the difference between the total of employees in Marketing and the total of employees in Sales, across the six month period?

A	B	C	D	E
21	26	31	28	35

A pie chart representing the number of crimes in a one month period

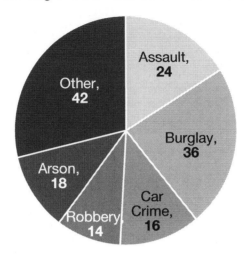

Question 21. How many crimes are there in total?

A	B	C	D	E
95	100	125	150	175

Question 22. Based on the total number of crimes, what percentage is the number of assault – related crimes?

A	B	C	D	E
9%	36%	16%	6%	13%

Question 23. What was the average number of crimes across the one month period?

A	B	C	D	E
25	50	15	20	45

Question 24. What is the difference between the lowest crime rate to the highest crime rate?

A	B	C	D	E
21	28	32	16	26

Question 25. What percentage is the number of burglary and arson-related crimes?

A	B	C	D	E
21%	55%	61%	42%	36%

Number of car accidents across the UK in a six month period

UK	Jan	Feb	Mar	April	May	June	Total
North	65	74	85	74	69	57	424
South	92	105	125	106	85	68	581
East	54	65	75	72	49	58	373
West	67	49	48	57	67	62	350
Total	278	293	333	309	270	245	1728

Question 26. What is the average number of car accidents across the 6 months in the South of the UK? To the nearest whole number.

A	B	C	D	E
87	89	91	95	97

Question 27. What month had the most car accidents?

A	B	C	D	E
January	February	March	April	May

Question 28. What percentage of the overall total was car accidents in the North? To the nearest whole number.

A	B	C	D	E
40%	25%	15%	60%	55%

Question 29. What is the difference between the month with the lowest number of car accidents and the month with the highest number of car accidents?

A	B	C	D	E
71	92	85	88	97

Question 30. What percentage of the total number of car accidents happened in January, April and May? To the nearest whole number.

A	B	C	D	E
51%	50%	54%	49%	48%

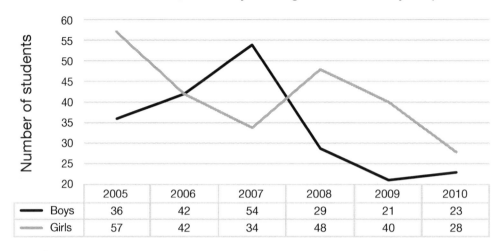

Number of A* students, both boys and girls across a 6 year period

	2005	2006	2007	2008	2009	2010
Boys	36	42	54	29	21	23
Girls	57	42	34	48	40	28

Question 31. In what year did the same number of A*s get achieved by girls and boys?

A	B	C	D	E
2005	2006	2007	2008	2009

Question 32. How many more A* grades did the boys achieve than the girls in 2007?

A	B	C	D	E
10	15	20	25	30

Question 33. How many A* grades did the girls achieve between 2005 and 2008?

A	B	C	D	E
136	172	179	181	183

Question 34. How many A* grades were achieved in 2009?

A	B	C	D	E
60	61	62	63	64

Question 35. In what year saw the biggest decrease from the year before for boys A*s?

A	B	C	D	E
2005	2006	2007	2008	2009

ANSWERS TO DATA INTERPRETATION

Q1. C

EXPLANATION = 50% of 40 = 20. No. of students who scored 20 and above in Maths = 36

Q2. D

EXPLANATION = 100 students, 52 students achieved marks 20 or above = 52%

Q3. A

EXPLANATION = no. of students with 30 or above in English = 19. No. of students with 20 or above in Science = 42. So 42 -19 = 23

Q4. B

EXPLANATION = 50% of 40 = 20. No. of students who scored 20 marks or above for average = 43. So, 100 – 43 = 57

Q5. C

EXPLANATION = scores of 10 or below = English = 9, Maths = 10, Science = 13.

Q6. D

EXPLANATION = 25 + 30 + 60 + 20 + 15 + 65 + 70 + 75 = 360 / 8 = 45 (thousand)

Q7. C

EXPLANATION = (20 - 60) / 60 = -66.66. To the nearest whole number = 67%. So there was a decline of 67%.

Q8. D

EXPLANATION = 65 - 15 / 15 = 3.333 x 100 = 333%

Q9. B

EXPLANATION = between 1997 and 1998, there was a decrease of 40,000 units. No other month saw a bigger decrease.

Q10. A

EXPLANATION = 75,000 – 15,000 = 60,000

Q11. D

Q12. C

Q13. B

EXPLANATION = 35 + 35 + 40 + 15 + 35 + 40 = 200

Q14. E

Q15. B

EXPLANATION = 45 + 35 + 30 + 20 + 15 = 145

Q16. D

EXPLANATION = 23 + 13 + 28 + 22 = 86

Q17. B

EXPLANATION = 24 + 11 + 22 + 13 = 70 / 4 = 17.5

Q18. C

EXPLANATION = 18 + 11 + 15 +13 + 13 + 18 = 88 / 6 = 14.6. To the nearest whole number = 15

Q19. B

EXPLANATION = 31 people were employed in the Sales department in April

Q20. D

EXPLANATION = Marketing 21 + 24 + 17 + 15 + 23 + 27 = 127. Sales 21 + 22 + 29 + 31 + 28 + 24 = 155. 155 − 127 = 28

Q21. D

EXPLANATION = 42 + 18 + 14 + 16 + 36 + 24 = 150

Q22. C

EXPLANATION = 24 / 150 x 100 = 16%

Q23. A

EXPLANATION = 150 / 6 = 25

Q24. B

EXPLANATION = 42 − 14 = 28

Q25. E

EXPLANATION = 36 + 18 = 54 / 150 x 100 = 36

Q26. E

EXPLANATION = 581 / 6 = 96.833. To the nearest whole number = 97

Q27. C

EXPLANATION = March had a total of 333 car accidents.

Q28. B

EXPLANATION = 424 / 1728 x 100 = 24.537. To the nearest whole number = 25%

Q29. D

EXPLANATION = 333 – 245 = 88

Q30. B

EXPLANATION = 278 + 309 + 270 = 857 / 1728 x 100 = 49.594. To the nearest whole number = 50%

Q31. B

EXPLANATION = in 2006, 42 girls and 42 boys achieved A* grades.

Q32. C

EXPLANATION = 54 – 34 = 20

Q33. D

EXPLANATION = 57 + 42 + 34 + 48 = 181

Q34. B

EXPLANATION = 21 + 40 = 61

Q35. D

EXPLANATION = between 2007 and 2008, there was a decrease of 25.

Now move on to the next section of the guide.

CHAPTER 5

(QUANTITATIVE REASONING)

ADMINISTRATIVE GRADE TESTS

Quantitative Reasoning is a type of psychometric testing that assesses a candidate's ability to deal with high levels of problem solving and mathematical formulas. Quantitative reasoning is used to assess your basic mathematical understanding and demonstrate your ability to apply your knowledge in relation to solutions and critical interpretation. There are 35 questions to answer in total. Carefully read each question before attempting to answer it.

We have deliberately provided you without a time frame in order for you to work through the questions carefully. You need to understand how these tests work and how to get to the correct answer. If you don't answer the questions correctly, you should take time to analyse your answers to understand where you went wrong.

Please circle your answer.

EXAMPLE

Question

There are two lists of numbers. One list contains 10 numbers, the average of which is 20. The second list contains 8 numbers. The average of this list is 22.5.

If the two lists are combined, what is the average of the numbers in the new list? To the nearest whole number.

How to work it out

- List 1 = 10 (numbers) x 20 (average) = 200
- List 2 = 8 (numbers) x 22.5 (average) 180
- 180 + 200 = 380
- 380 / (10 + 8) = 21.111
- To the nearest whole number = 21

Answer

21

Question 1

A school trip to Dover Castle is taking place. There are 87 students attending the trip. For every 6 students, 1 adult is needed. Each coach can accommodate 54 people, how many coaches will be needed to accommodate everyone?

A	B	C	D	E
1	2	3	4	5

Question 2

Kylie earns £19,600 per annum. Her husband earns 33% more than her income. How much is her husband earning?

A	B	C	D	E
£24,500	£27,070	£26,068	£21,320	£33,125

Question 3

At 20 mph, how long does it take to travel 68 miles? Time = Distance / Speed. Give your answer in hour and minutes.

A	B	C	D	E
2 hrs and 4 mins	3 hrs and 24 mins	4 hours	3 hours	1 hr and 46 mins

Question 4

Joe earns £550 a week. He gets taxed 15%. How much does Joe earn if he takes off what he will be taxed?

A	B	C	D	E
£467.50	£432.50	£413.50	£421.50	£428.50

Question 5

Peter earns £600 a week, without taking tax into consideration. His tax is £78 per week. What percentage is his tax in terms of his weekly income?

A	B	C	D	E
9%	11%	21%	28%	13%

Question 6

A company makes a profit of £18,500 in 2012. In 2013, their profit was 17% more than the previous year. What was the total profit for the company in 2013?

A	B	C	D	E
£23,450	£25,000	£21,645	£22,456	£20,026

Question 7

Teaching staff at a secondary school has the ratio of male to female staff as 1:4. If there are 7 male staff at the school, how many female staff are there?

A	B	C	D	E
22	24	26	28	30

Question 8

There are two lists of numbers. One list contains 11 numbers, the average of which is 36. The second list contains 13 numbers and has the average of 41. If the two lists are combined, what is the average of the numbers in the new list? To the nearest whole number.

A	B	C	D	E
36	37	38	39	40

Question 9

Brian spends 9 hours a day at work. He works five days a week. Brian spends a third of his time meeting with his clientele base. How much time does Brian spend a week with his clientele base?

A	B	C	D	E
15 hours	22 hours	25.30 hours	15.30 hours	21 hours

Question 10

If a printer can produce 180 pieces of printed documents in one hour, how many printed documents can be printed with three printers in 35 minutes?

A	B	C	D	E
105	315	210	405	275

Question 11

A wallet contains three £10 notes, four £5 notes, one £20 note, a 20p, a 5p, two 2p's and 1p. How much money does the wallet contain?

A	B	C	D	E
£70.50	£56.70	£68.30	£68.00	£70.30

Question 12

Ryan is going on holiday. He needs to change up his money into euros. The exchange rate for pounds to euros is 1:1.9. If Ryan changes up £850, how many euros will he get?

A	B	C	D	E
1,208 euros	1,315 euros	1,615 euros	2,000 euros	960 euros

Question 13

A kitchen floor needs to be tiled. Per tile costs £1.79. How much would it cost if the kitchen needed 51 tiles?

A	B	C	D	E
£91.29	£93.38	£78.41	£101.36	£97.52

Question 14

A farmland area is measured to be 220m in length by 80m in width. What is the approximate area of the field in hectares? 1 hectare = 10,000m2 = 2.47 acres

A	B	C	D	E
17 hectares	1.76 hectares	176 hectares	17.6 hectares	7.67 hectares

Question 15

A rectangle has a length of 13cm and a width of 8.5cm. What is the difference between the rectangle's perimeter and the rectangle's area?

A	B	C	D	E
63.75	61.5	67.5	60.5	61.5

Question 16

Thirty per cent of staff at a school are part time. We know that there are 63 staff members who are full time. What is the number of staff that are part time?

A	B	C	D	E
27	25	24	29	21

Question 17

There are three lists of numbers. One list contains 7 numbers, the average of which is 56. The second list contains 15 numbers and has an average of 72. The third list has 9 numbers and has an average number of 36. If the three lists are combined, what is the average of the numbers in the new list? To the nearest whole number.

A	B	C	D	E
53	55	57	58	60

Question 18

A recipe for flapjacks requires 320g of oats. This makes 18 flapjacks. What quantity of oats would be needed to make 28 flapjacks? To the nearest whole number.

A	B	C	D	E
491g	493g	498g	500g	503g

Question 19

Sarah is 8 years old. Her brother Matthew is 12 years old. Their grandmother gives them £160 which is to be divided between the ratio of their ages. How much money does Matthew get?

A	B	C	D	E
£34	£96	£64	£58	£62

Question 20

In a school year, the number of left-handed people to right-handed people is 1:8. If there are 135 people in the school year, how many people are right-handed?

A	B	C	D	E
110	85	36	120	55

Question 21

The following graph shows Emma's testing scores in her first year of university.

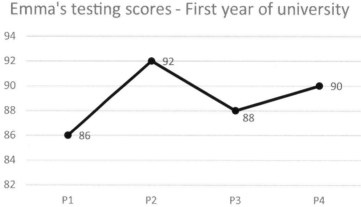

In her second year, Emma scored 84 points in P5. What is the difference between her P5 score in her second year and her average project score in the first year?

A	B	C	D	E
1	2	3	4	5

Question 22

The total estimated amount of spending in a household is £489 a week. In 2013, it was estimated that 26% of the money was spent on housing, 20% on transportation and 21% on food. In total, how much was spent in a family household on housing, transport and food on a weekly basis?

A	B	C	D	E
£317.64	£327.63	£357.85	£395.71	£315.17

Question 23

Government spending on a family claiming Basic Working Tax Credits and Severe Disability Tax Credits was £1,940 and £1,255 in 2014. In the same year, Government also spent £545 for Child Tax Credits. It was estimated that the Government was eligible to pay 70% of the total cost to the family for those Tax Credits.

How much does the Government have to pay the family claiming Basic Working Tax Credits, Severe Disability Credits and Child Tax Credits?

A	B	C	D	E
£2618	£2816	£2281	£2861	£6281

Question 24

A new company analyses their profits for the first two years. The profit for 2010 was £1,350. If the profit increases by 125%, how much profit does the company make in 2011? To the nearest whole number.

A	B	C	D	E
£1,688	£2,018	£6,188	£6,161	£1,681

Question 25

The following table shows the percentage of nickel in two coins.

COIN	WEIGHT	NICKEL
50p coin	8g	25%
20p coin	5g	16%

If both the coins are made only of nickel and copper, what is the difference between the weight of copper present in the 50p coin and the weight of copper in the 20p coin?

A	B	C	D	E
1g	0.8g	0.08g	1.8g	2.8g

Question 26

Michael bikes to school every weekday. It takes him 25 minutes to get from his house to school. Assuming his ride home is the same time, how long does Michael spend biking to and from school each week? Give your answer in hours and minutes.

A	B	C	D	E
3 hours and 30 mins	4 hours and 5 mins	4 hours and 10 mins	4 hours and 35 mins	3 hours and 55 mins

Question 27

A business has a total of 5,200 employees. Due to financial difficulty, the business has no option but to let go 25% of its employees. How many employees remain at the business?

A	B	C	D	E
1,300	2,600	3,900	4,000	4,050

Question 28

A charity bike ride is taking place. The bike ride is 48 kilometres long. If 1 kilometre is approximately 0.6 miles, approximately how many miles will they be riding?

A	B	C	D	E
22.4 miles	28.8 miles	29.3 miles	30 miles	30.6 miles

Question 29

A secondary school has 120 pupils in Year 7. In Year 7, 42 pupils have a reading age below the recommended reading level. What percentage of pupils have a reading age below the recommended reading level?

A	B	C	D	E
30%	35%	40%	45%	60%

Question 30

Two business classes are merged together for the day. There are 25 people from business class A and 30 people from business class B. What is the ratio of people from business class A to business class B? In its simplest form.

A	B	C	D	E
5:6	4:6	1:5	2:5	3:4

Question 31

A parking space at the train station for a weekly ticket costs £28.00. The price of the ticket goes up by 13%. What is the new price of a weekly parking ticket at the train station?

A	B	C	D	E
£29.85	£30.64	£30.84	£31.64	£32.50

Question 32

Bill earns £54,000 pa. In addition to his main salary, he also receives a 12% bonus of his annual wage every 3 months. How much does Bill earn for his bonuses across a one year period?

A	B	C	D	E
£42,120	£31,245	£21,325	£25,920	£25,725

Question 33

A lady has been prescribed medication by her doctor. She is prescribed a 10.5 fluid ounce bottle of medication with the instructions to take 0.25 fluid ounces three times a day. How many days does she have to take the medication for?

A	B	C	D	E
7 days	10 days	12 days	13 days	14 days

Question 34

Matthew earns £30,000 per annum. His wife earns 18% more than his monthly income. How much does Matthew's wife earn in five months?

A	B	C	D	E
£12,000	£5,200	£14,750	£22,500	£18,600

Question 35

Rachel drives at an average speed of 45 mph for 135 miles. How long does the journey take Rachel?

A	B	C	D	E
2 hours and 20 mins	3 hours	3 hours and 10 mins	3 hours and 35 mins	4 hours

ANSWERS TO QUANTITATIVE REASONING

Q1. B

EXPLANATION = 1 adult to every 6 children. 87 / 6 = 14.5. So you would need 15 adults. 15 + 87 = 102. Each coach can accommodate 54 people, meaning 2 coaches would be needed

Q2. C

EXPLANATION = 19,600 / 100 x 33 = 6,468. 6,468 + 19,600 = 26,068

Q3. B

EXPLANATION = 68 / 20. The denominator (bottom half of the fraction) must go into 60 (minutes). So, 20 goes into 60 three times. So 68 x 3 =204 minutes or 3 hrs and 24 mins

Q4. A

EXPLANATION = 550 / 100 x 15 = 82.50. 550 − 82.50 = £467.50

Q5. E

EXPLANATION = 78 / 600 x 100 = 13

Q6. C

EXPLANATION = 18,500 / 100 x 17 = 3,145. 3,145 + 18,500 = 21,645

Q7. D

EXPLANATION = 1:4 male to female. 7 males = 7 x 4 = 28

Q8. D

EXPLANATION = 11 x 36 = 396. 13 x 41 = 533. 533 + 396 = 929 / (11 + 13) = 38.708. To the nearest whole number = 39

Q9. A

EXPLANATION = 9 x 5 = 45. 45 / 3 = 15 hours

Q10. B

EXPLANATION = 180 / 60 (minutes) = 3. 3 x 35 = 105. 105 x 3 = 315

Q11. E

EXPLANATION = 10 + 10 + 10 + 5 + 5 + 5 + 5 + 20 + 0.2 + 0.05 + 0.02 + 0.02 + 0.01 = 70.30

Q12. C

EXPLANATION = for every 1 pound = 1.9 euros. So £850 = 850 x 1.9 = 1615 euros

Q13. A

EXPLANATION = 1.79 x 51 = 91.29

Q14. B

EXPLANATION = 220 x 80 = 17,600 m2. 17,600 / 10,000 = 1.76 hectares

Q15. C

EXPLANATION = Area = 13 x 8.5 = 110.5. Perimeter = 13 + 13 + 8.5 + 8.5 = 43. So, the difference = 110.5 – 43 = 67.5

Q16. A

EXPLANATION = 63 x 100 / 70 = 90. 90 is how many staff members there are in total. So, 90 / 100 x 30 = 27

Q17. D

EXPLANATION = 7 x 56 = 392. 15 x 72 = 1080. 9 x 36 = 324. So, 324 + 1080 + 392 = 1796. The number of total numbers = 7 + 15 + 9 = 31. 1796 / 31 = 57.935. To the nearest whole number = 58

Q18. C

EXPLANATION = 320 / 18 x 28 = 497.777. To the nearest whole number = 498

Q19. B

EXPLANATION = 160 / 20 x 12 = 96

Q20. D

EXPLANATION = 135 / 9 x 8 = 120

Q21. E

EXPLANATION = 86 + 92 + 88 + 90 = 356 / 4 = 89. So, the difference between Emma's average score in her first year (89) with her P5 score (84) = 5

Q22. B

EXPLANATION = 489 / 100 x 26 = 127.14. 489 / 100 x 20 = 97.80. 489 / 100 x 21 = 102.69. So, 127.14 + 97.80 + 102.69 = 327.63

Q23. A

EXPLANATION = 1940 + 1255 + 545 = 3740. 3740 / 100 x 70 = 2618

Q24. A

EXPLANATION = 1350 / 100 x 125 = 1687.5. To the nearest whole number = 1688

Q25. D

EXPLANATION = 8 / 100 x 75 = 6. 5 / 100 x 84 = 4.2. So, 6 – 4.2 = 1.8

Q26. C

EXPLANATION = 25 x 2 = 50 (mins per day). 50 x 5 = 250 (mins). 250 mins = 4 hours and 10 mins

Q27. C

EXPLANATION = 5200 / 100 x 25 = 1300 (people who are being let go). So, 5200 – 1300 = 3900

Q28. B

EXPLANATION = 1 km = 0.6 miles. So, 48 km = 48 x 0.6 = 28.8 miles

Q29. B

EXPLANATION = 42 / 120 x 100 = 35

Q30. A

EXPLANATION = you have to find a number that both 25 and 30 go into. 5 goes into both. So, 25 / 5 = 5. 30 / 5 = 6. So the ratio is 5:6. This is in its simplest form because 5 is a prime number and therefore cannot be lowered.

Q31. D

EXPLANATION = 28 / 100 x 13 = 3.64. So, 28 + 3.64 = 31.64

Q32. D

EXPLANATION = 54000 / 100 x 12 = 6480. 6480 x 4 = £25,920

Q33. E

EXPLANATION = 0.25 x 3 = 0.75 (a day). 10.5 / 0.75 = 14

Q34. C

EXPLANATION = 30000 / 12 = 2500 (husbands monthly income). Wife earns 18% more = 2500 / 100 x 18 = 450 + 2500 = 2950 (wife's monthly income). So, 2950 x 5 = 14750

Q35. B

EXPLANATION = 135 / 45 = 3 hours

Now move on to the next section of the guide.

CHAPTER 6

(CORRECT SENTENCES)

ADMINISTRATIVE GRADE TESTS

The Civil Service tests will measure a candidate's ability to identify errors in terms of sentence structures and language. The sub-section 'correct sentences' primarily deals with four key aspects. A candidate needs to be able to analyse and correctly use:

- Basic grammar.
- Sentence structure.
- Choice of words (diction).
- Idiomatic expressions.

These four key elements will allow a candidate to spot a mistake, based on one of the key elements as stated. For this section, you will be presented with 30 questions, which will have four possible choices to choose from.

We have deliberately provided you without a time frame in order for you to work through the questions carefully. You need to understand how these tests work and how to get to the correct answer. If you don't answer the questions correctly, you should take the time to analyse your answers to understand where you went wrong.

EXAMPLE

Question

A. Graduates are finding it more difficult to find a job that is relevant to there studies.

B. Graduates our finding it more difficult to find a job that its releveant to their studies.

C. Graduates are finding it more difficult to find a job that is relevant to their studies.

D. Graduate's are finding it more difficult to find a job that is relevant to their studies.

How to work it out

A – Uses the wrong 'there' so therefore is incorrect.

B – Uses the wrong 'our' and 'relevant' is spelt incorrectly.

C – Provides the most logical sentence structure, with correct grammar and punctuation.

D – 'Graduate's' should not have an apostrophe and is therefore incorrect.

Answer

C

For the following questions, identify which of the options is correct in terms of the correct sentencing. Pay attention to grammar, spelling, punctuation and sentence structure.

Indicate your answer by writing the letter of the correct answer in the answer box provided.

Question 1

A – If your looking for a place to stay, there is a nearby hotel.

B – If you're looking for a place to stay, their is a nearby hotel.

C – If you're looking for a place to stay, there are a nearby hotel.

D – If you're looking for a place to stay, there is a nearby hotel.

Answer

Question 2

A – We will give you a call later on today.

B – We will be given you a call later on today.

C – We will give you a called later on today.

D – We will give you a call on later today.

Answer

Question 3

A – I wish you the very best of luck with all you're future endeavours.
B – I wishes you the very best of luck will all your endeavours into the future.
C - I wish you the very best of luck with all your future endeavours.
D – I wish the very best of luck to you for all your future endevours.

Answer [   ]

Question 4

A – Unfortunately for us, are flight is been delayed.
B – For us unfortunately is our flight been delayed.
C – For us it is unfortunately that are flight have been delayed.
D - Unfortunately for us, our flight has been delayed.

Answer [   ]

Question 5

A – Please rite your name and address on the documents provided.
B – Please write your name and address on the documents provided.
C – Please right your name and address on the documents provided.
D – Please write on the documents provide your name and address.

Answer [   ]

Question 6

A – We will be in contact with you shortly.
B – We will be in contact with you shortley.
C – We will in contact be with you shortly.
D – Shortly will we be in contact with you.

Answer

Question 7

A – Yours sincerity.
B – Your's sincerely.
C – Yours sincerely.
D – You're sincerely.

Answer

Question 8

A – I regret to inform you that you did not get chosen for the internship.
B – I inform to regret you that you did not get chosen for the internship.
C – I regret to inform you, that, you did not get chose for the internship.
D – I regret to inform your that you did not get chosen for the internship.

Answer

Question 9

A – When I go to university, I will have not enough time for reading for pleasure.

B – When I goes to university, I will not have enough time to read for pleasure.

C – When I go to university, I will not have enough time to read for pleasure.

D – When I go to university and I will not has enough time for reading for pleasure.

Answer

Question 10

A – The police has a new suspect.

B – The police have a new suspect.

C – The police as a new suspect.

D – The police not have a new suspect.

Answer

Question 11

A – The most important thing is to be yourself.

B – The most important think is to be yourself.

C – The most importance, is to be yourself.

D – The most important thing is to be your self.

Answer

Question 12

A – We are all so proud of what you have achievement.
B – We our all so proud of what you have achieved.
C – We are all so proud of what you has achieved.
D - We are all so proud of what you have achieved.

Answer

Question 13

A – We our pleased to inform you that your application was successful.
B – We are pleased to inform you that your application was successful.
C – We are please to of informed you that you're application was successful.
D – We are pleased to inform you that you application is successful.

Answer

Question 14

A – We promise to notify you of any changes to your flight.
B – We promises to notify yourself of any changes to your flight.
C – We promise to notify you of any changed to your flight.
D – We promise to notify you of any changed to your flight's.

Answer

Question 15

A – They take a walk along the riverside and decided to have lunch in the country pub.

B – They took a walk along the riverside and decided to have lunch in the country pub.

C – They took a walk along the riverside and decided to has lunch in the country pub.

D – They taken a walk along the riverside and decided to as lunch in the country pub.

Answer

Question 16

A – I was teaching my neice how to play the piano.

B – I was teaching my niece how two play the piano.

C - I was teaching my niece how to play the piano.

D – I was teaching my niece how to played the piano.

Answer

Question 17

A – My husband and I got married last December just before Christmas.

B – My husband and me got married last December just before Christmas.

C – My husband and myself getting married last December just before Christmas.

D – My husband and I gotten married last December just before Christmas.

Answer

Question 18

A – I am currently supervising an team of advertisers to come up with an exciting new idea.

B – I are currently supervising a team of advertisers to come up with an exciting new idea.

C – I am currently supervising a team of advertisers to come up with a exciting new idea.

D - I am currently supervising a team of advertisers to come up with an exciting new idea.

Answer

Question 19

A – I am afraid of losing my job because of the mistake I made earlier.

B – I am afraid off losing my job because of the mistake I made earlier.

C – I am afraid of losing my job because of the mistake I make earlier.

D – I am afraid of losing my job and the mistake I made earlier.

Answer

Question 20

A – My daughter loves playing outside and jumping in puddles.

B – My daughter love playing outside and jumping in puddles.

C – My daughter love's playing outside and jumping in puddles.

D – My daughter loves played outside and jumping in puddles.

Answer

Question 21

A – My family is very passionate about recycling and helping the environment.

B – My family are very passion about recycling and helping the environment.

C – My family are very passionate about recycling but helping the environment.

D – My family are very passionate about recycling and helping the environment.

Answer

Question 22

A – I have an interview today. I is really nervous.

B – I have an interview today. I am really nervous.

C – I has an interview today. I am really nervous.

D – I as an interview today. I am really nervous.

Answer

Question 23

A – The chicken is the most common species of bird found in the world.

B – The chicken is the most common specie of bird found in the world.

C – The chicken are the most common species of birds found in the world.

D – The chicken is the more common specie of bird found in the world.

Answer

Question 24

A – The ostrich are the largest's bird in the world which also produces the largest eggs.

B – The ostrich is the largest bird in the world within also produces the largest eggs.

C – The ostrich is the largest bird in the world which also produces the largest eggs.

D – The ostrich is the largest bird in world also produces the largest eggs.

Answer

Question 25

A – People need to look after there body by exercising and eating healthily.

B – People need to look after their body by exercising and eating healthy.

C – People need to looked after their body by exercising and eating healthily.

D – People needed to look after their body by exercising and eating healthily.

Answer

Question 26

A – Further information is available to you via our website.

B – Further information are available to you via our website.

C – Further information is available to you via are website.

D – Further information is availability to you via our website.

Answer

Question 27

A – A lot of graduate's decide to take a gap year and go travelling.

B – A lots of graduates decide to take a gap year and go travelling.

C - A lot of graduates decide to take a gap year and go travelling.

D – A lot of graduates decides to take a gap year and go traveling.

Answer

Question 28

A – If you purchase broken goods, you have the write to take it back.

B – If you purchases broken goods, you have the rite to take it back.

C – If you purchase broken goods, you has the right to take it back.

D - If you purchase broken goods, you have the right to take it back.

Answer

Question 29

A – Gareth has a trial at a football club. If he does well, he could play professionally.

B – Gareth have a trial at a football club. If he do well, he could play professional.

C – Gareth has a trial at a football club. If he do well, he could play professionally.

D – Gareth has a trial at a football club. If he does well, he could play professionalism.

Answer

Question 30

A – Parents are responsible for teaching there children the difference between right and wrong.

B – Parents is responsible for teaching their children the difference between right and wrong.

C – Parents are responsible for teaching their children the difference between right and wrong.

D – Parents have responsibilities teach their children difference of right and wrong.

Answer

ANSWERS TO CORRECT SENTENCES

Q1. D

Q2. A

Q3. C

Q4. D

Q5. B

Q6. A

Q7. C

Q8. A

Q9. C

Q10. B

Q11. A

Q12. D

Q13. B

Q14. A

Q15. B

Q16. C

Q17. A

Q18. D

Q19. A

Q20. A

Q21. D

Q22. B

Q23. A

Q24. C

Q25. B

Q26. A

Q27. C

Q28. D

Q29. A

Q30. C

Now move on to the next section of the guide.

CHAPTER 7

(WORD SWAP)

ADMINISTRATIVE GRADE TESTS

The tests in this section are called 'word swap'. You will be given a sentence, of which two words will be swapped with one another. Your aim is to work out which two words have been swapped, and have replaced one another's positions within the sentence.

Read the sentence carefully and work out which two words are in the incorrect place. It may be quite difficult to extract the words from the sentence; try reading them out loud if it helps. Reading them out loud will help you understand the sentence structure and determine whether or not the sentence makes sense.

We have deliberately provided you without a time frame in order for you to work through the questions carefully. You need to understand how these tests work and how to get to the correct answer. If you don't answer the questions correctly, you should take the time to analyse your answers and understand where you went wrong.

EXAMPLE

Question

Hearing music can be a result of listening to loud loss and having ear pieces in.

How to work it out

- If you read the sentence out loud, you will notice that it does not make sense.
- Hearing **music** can be a result of listening to loud **loss** and having ear pieces in.
- If swap the **highlighted** words around, the sentence makes sense.

Answer

Music and loss

Question 1

Having an operation will lack in loss of muscle strength and will result movement.

Answer

Question 2

The elderly like to memories about their past to not only make conversation, but keep their reminisce alive.

Answer

Question 3

Minimum benefits has now been raised to over £5.00 in 2014, which wage employees aged 18 to 20.

Answer

Question 4

Doctors recommended us to eat the advise amount of fruit and vegetables to ensure a healthier lifestyle.

Answer

Question 5

Children from the ages of 5 months to six years are at a necessary developing stage. It is important that they engage with the critical learning skills to ensure maximum potential.

Answer

Question 6

People who drink and drive not only put their lives in risk, but also puts other people's lives at danger.

Answer [   ]

Question 7

Learning a foreign language at school not only broadens a child's lifestyles prospects but allows them to engage with different cultures and learning.

Answer [   ]

Question 8

The health benefits of taking omega 3 is suggested by improve mental health to insulating nerve cells in the brain allowing for better communication.

Answer [   ]

Question 9

Smoking cigarettes are extremely bad for your health, especially if you are asthmatic. If you trigger asthma, tobacco smoke can have an attack or even make an asthma attack worse.

Answer [   ]

Question 10

In contemporary generation, technology has become increasingly popular, particularly for the younger society.

Answer [   ]

Question 11

Sometimes, bringing home a baby new-born makes dogs particularly cautious, confused and beg for attention.

Answer

Question 12

Applying to universities is challenging and incentive for every student involved. It takes a great deal of commitment and time-consuming to work through the long-winded process.

Answer

Question 13

The doctor prescribed sleep remedied to help me drift off to sleep. He claimed that the remedies are completely organic. They are made from natural and harmless substances which allow you to slowly drift off to sleep.

Answer

Question 14

It will be on Ryan's conscious if she does not remain conscience.

Answer

Question 15

We are likely to be late so we should probably let your parents know we are behind running schedule.

Answer

Question 16

Whether forecasters have a difficult job at predicting the outcome. Weather they are right or wrong will only be known on the day.

Answer [   ]

Question 17

It would be foolish to venture outside and the thundery storm in torrential downpour.

Answer [   ]

Question 18

The younger generation should show respect courtesy and common in regards to their elders.

Answer [   ]

Question 19

Our neighbourhood our completely safe, we have is own safety procedures and regulations firmly in place.

Answer [   ]

Question 20

A recent study performed on mice indicate that drinking apple juice could fight Alzheimer's away and keep aging effects of the brain.

Answer [   ]

Question 21

Lack of damage to the brain for 5 to 10 minutes results in permanent brain oxygen.

Answer

Question 22

Your brain uses 20% of the total oxygen of amount and blood in your whole entire body.

Answer

Question 23

The brain power on the same amount of operates as a 10-watt light bulb.

Answer

Question 24

There are more living forms living on a person's skin than there are people life on the planet.

Answer

Question 25

It is obvious quite that the applicant has an enthusiastic approach and bubbly personality.

Answer

Question 26

Teaching pre-schoolers sign language helps ensuring brain development. Using sign language uses both the left and right hemisphere of the brain, stimulate creativity and intellectual ability.

Answer

Question 27

Take each step and it comes as try not to think about the long run.

Answer

Question 28

You should not take life for moment. Live life in the granted.

Answer

Question 29

It is impossible to predict your future. Try not to worry about the present and enjoy your time in the future.

Answer

Question 30

The opportunity of going to university outweigh the reasons not to go. It provides a life benefits for a young person to experience and gain knowledge in something that they love to do.

Answer

ANSWERS TO WORD SWAP

Q1. Lack / result

Q2. Memories / reminisce

Q3. Benefits / wage

Q4. Recommended / advise

Q5. Necessary / critical

Q6. Risk / danger

Q7. Learning / lifestyles

Q8. By / to

Q9. Trigger / have

Q10. Generation / society

Q11. Baby / new-born

Q12. Incentive / time-consuming

Q13. Organic / harmless

Q14. Conscience / conscious

Q15. Running / behind

Q16. Weather / whether

Q17. And / in

Q18. Respect / common

Q19. Our / is

Q20. Keep / fight

Q21. Damage / oxygen

Q22. Oxygen / amount

Q23. Operates / power

Q24. Life / living

Q25. Obvious / quite

Q26. Ensuring / stimulate

Q27. As / and

Q28. Moment / granted

Q29. Future / present

Q30. Benefits / opportunity

Now move on to the next section of the guide.

CHAPTER 8

(MISSING WORDS)

ADMINISTRATIVE GRADE TESTS

For this section on 'Missing Words', you will be presented with a sentence. Each sentence will have two words missing. Your job is simple – to fill in the missing words with the words provided. The possible answer options have two words; the group with the right answer will have the two words in order in which they follow in the sentence.

You may think this test is easy; but be careful! The test is designed to trick you by using words that look or sound similar. Pay attention to spelling in particular!

We have deliberately provided you without a time frame in order for you to work through the questions carefully. You need to understand how these tests work and how to get to the correct answer. If you don't answer the questions correctly, you should take time to analyse your answers to understand where you went wrong.

Please circle the correct answer.

EXAMPLE

Question

It was _____ choice where they went to college. _____ are some great colleges to choose from.

How to work it out

- Their = is the possessive form. In other words it indicates something belonging to someone.
- There = is a place. I.e. not here. Also used when saying there 'is' or there 'are'

Answer

Their / there

Question 1

Peter won an award for outstanding achievement. He .... the award ....

A	B	C	D
Excepted / Grascious	Accepted / Graciously	Expected / Gracily	Eccepted / Graciously

Question 2

The evidence .... the jury to reach a unanimous ....

A	B	C	D
Led / Decisive	Lead / Decision	Led / Decision	Leed / Decishion

Question 3

The .... of the school enforced many .... to ensure an effective code of conduct.

A	B	C	D
Principal / Principles	Principles / Principal	Princepal / Principals	Principle / Principles

Question 4

She .... the piano every day. .... makes perfect.

A	B	C	D
Practices / Practices	Practices / Practices	Practises / Practice	Practises / Practisce

Question 5

Two journalists went missing and are .... dead. You can .... that the stormy conditions made them lose their way.

A	B	C	D
Assumed / Presume	Assumed / Assume	Presumed / Presume	Presumed / Assiume

Question 6

James had a way of .... Rebecca but never saying her name. He really liked her. After three years, Rebecca still .... James.

A	B	C	D
Eluding / Alluded	Alluding / Eluded	Eluding / Eluded	Alluded / Eluding

Question 7

To .... do you wish to speak? Do they .... what this is in reference to?

A	B	C	D
Hue / Know	Who / No	Whom / No	Whom / Know

Question 8

I want my father to walk me down the .... at my wedding. My fiancé and I are getting married on the .... of Fernando.

A	B	C	D
Eyeal / Aisle	Aisle / Isle	Isle / Aisle	Ale / Aisle

Question 9

We took a walk in the .... evening. Walking along the beach I thought someone was following us. I thought I was going ....

A	B	C	D
Balmy / Barny	Barney / Balmey	Barmy / Barny	Balmy / Barmy

Question 10

I can't .... to think of someone looking through the window and seeing me .... naked.

A	B	C	D
Bear / Bare	Bear / Bear	Bare / Bear	Bair / Bear

Question 11

The Government have .... that thousands of people may .... their job.

A	B	C	D
Infer / Loose	Infer / Lose	Implied / Lose	Inplied / Loose

Question 12

A child is a .... of its mother and father. My children are .... on me as their parent.

A	B	C	D
Dependant / Dependent	Dependent / Dependent	Dependent / Dependant	Deependent / Dependernt

Question 13

Ryan got angry and .... the first punch. The boys stood there fighting whilst others .... round to watch.

A	B	C	D
Though / Gathered	Through / Gathers	Threw / Gathered	Thorough / Gavered

Question 14

My family decided to take a long road trip down a small remote and .... route. It was .... having to sit in the car with my brothers for hours.

A	B	C	D
Torturous / Tortureous	Torturous / Tortuous	Tortoise / Tortuous	Tortuous / Torturous

Question 15

It is important to get .... in case anything happens. It is fundamentally important to .... that my family are well looked after.

A	B	C	D
Ensured / Insured	Insured / ensure	Insure / Insurance	Onshore / Ensure

Question 16

A business cannot afford to be .... about security. They need to demonstrate high levels of safety and security ....

A	B	C	D
Complaisant / Procedures	Complacent / Proceedures	Complaisant / Prosedures	Complacent / Procedures

Question 17

The police are working on a .... that teaches them how to .... a potentially dangerous situation.

A	B	C	D
Scheam / Defuse	Scheme / Defuse	Sceme / Diffuse	Scheme / Diffuse

Question 18

We made some .... inquiries and had to .... into the office after hours.

A	B	C	D
Discreet / Break	Discrete / Break	Discrete / Brake	Discreet / Brake

Question 19

.... interesting to see whether or not students do .... homework.

A	B	C	D
It / Their	Its / They're	Its' / There	It's / Their

Question 20

Some companies are thinking of conducting team .... as .... to individual appraisals.

A	B	C	D
Apprise / Opposed	Appraisals / Apposed	Appraisals / Opposed	Appraisals / Apposed

Question 21

The _____ of traffic was going nowhere. It seems a car has collided with a _____ vehicle.

A	B	C	D
Cue / Stationary	Queue / Stationary	Queue / Stationery	Cue / Stationairy

Question 22

The man seemed _____ and doubtful about the boys who _____ hooded tops in his shop.

A	B	C	D
Sceptical / Wore	Septic / Wore	Scepticism / Wear	Sceptical / Where

Question 23

The _____ from the shop was torn in half. She had to _____ it back together so she could return an item.

A	B	C	D
Recipe / Peace	Recipe / Peice	Receet / Pierce	Receipt / Piece

Question 24

It proved difficult for the man to come to terms with the _____ loss of his beloved _____ .

A	B	C	D
Tragedy / Spouse	Tradgic / Sphouse	Tragic / Spouse	Tragick / Spowse

Question 25

A _____ of drunken football fans came stumbling into the pub and were extremely _____ .

A	B	C	D
Horde / Aloud	Hored / Aloud	Hoard / Loud	Horde / Loud

Question 26

After a _____ examination, her test results _____ all clear.

A	B	C	D
Through / Wear	Thought / Were	Thorough / Were	Thorough / Where

Question 27

Strikes were _____ in the armed forces. It is specified that the armed forces are under a strong command of _____ .

A	B	C	D
Proscribed / Responsibility	Prescribed / Responsibility	Proscribe / Responsibilitie	Prescribe / Responsability

Question 28

He would have gone to prison had it not been for _____ _____ .

A	B	C	D
Militating / Circumstances	Mitigating / Circumstances	Mitigating / Sircumstances	Militate / Circumstanses

Question 29

The government decides to _____ a new policy in hope to _____ people's wellbeing.

A	B	C	D
Adopt / Enhance	Adapt / Enhance	Adopt / Inhance	Adapt / Enharnce

Question 30

Some people say it is never _____ late to follow your dreams. You need to believe in yourself and have the confidence to _____ .

A	B	C	D
To / Succeed	Two / Succeed	Too / Succeed	To / Success

ANSWERS TO MISSING WORDS

Q1. B – Accepted / graciously

Q2. C – Led / decision

Q3. A – Principal / principles

Q4. C – Practises / practice

Q5. D – Presumed / assume

Q6. B – Alluding / eluded

Q7. D – Whom / know

Q8. B – Aisle / isle

Q9. D – Balmy / barmy

Q10. A – Bear / bare

Q11. C – Implied / lose

Q12. A – Dependant / dependent

Q13. C – Threw / gathered

Q14. D – Tortuous / torturous

Q15. B – Insured / ensure

Q16. D – Complacent / procedures

Q17. B – Scheme / defuse

Q18. A – Discreet / break

Q19. D – It's / their

Q20. C – Appraisals / opposed

Q21. B – Queue / stationary

Q22. A – Sceptical / wore

Q23. D – Receipt / piece

Q24. C – Tragic / spouse

Q25. D – Horde / loud

Q26. C – Thorough / were

Q27. A – Proscribed / responsibility

Q28. B – Mitigating circumstances

Q29. A – Adopt / enhance

Q30. C – Too / succeed

Now move on to the next section of the guide.

CHAPTER 9

(SPEED AND ACCURACY)

ADMINISTRATIVE GRADE TESTS

Speed and accuracy questions are designed to test your ability to work under pressure in a small time scale. The term 'speed and accuracy' is self-explanatory. It will look at not only how capable you are of answering the questions quickly, but also how well you answer them accurately.

For this test, you are required to compare numbers and letters that have been laid out in pairs; spread across two columns. Each column contains four pairs, and your task is to analyse the data and indicate which numbers and letters from column 1 are identical to those in column 2. You are given five possible choices: all four pairs are identical, only three pairs are identical, 2 pairs are identical, 1 pair is identical or none.

We have deliberately provided you without a time frame in order for you to work through the questions carefully. You need to understand how these tests work and how to get to the correct answer. If you don't answer the questions correctly, you should take time to analyse your answers to understand where you went wrong.

Please circle the correct answer.

EXAMPLE

Question

44we1	44we1
1ol23d	1ol23d
dd2er	dd2er
bi61c	bi6ic

How to work it out

- You can notice that in column 1, only three pairs match up to the pairs found in column 2.

44we1	44we1 = identical
1ol23d	1ol23d = identical
dd2er	dd2er = identical
bi61c	bi6ic = NOT identical

Answer

3 pairs

Question 1

a4er7	afer7
b0ef5	b0ef5
ggil7	gg1l7
t533o	t533o

A	B	C	D	E
All 4 pairs	3 pairs	2 pairs	1 pair	None

Question 2

o0ewk	o0ewk
mwa4k	mwa4k
b43et	b43et
tt9k5	tt9k5

A	B	C	D	E
All 4 pairs	3 pairs	2 pairs	1 pair	None

Question 3

34019	34091
er8rm	er8rm
v84nf	v48nf
d633m	d336m

A	B	C	D	E
All 4 pairs	3 pairs	2 pairs	1 pair	None

Question 4

m8e7d   me87d

84me4   84me4

trac4   trac4

8b3k5   8b3k5

A	B	C	D	E
All 4 pairs	3 pairs	2 pairs	1 pair	None

Question 5

l7fmt   lf7tm

r4p1a   r4p11

g80o2   g8o02

flba0   fbaa0

A	B	C	D	E
All 4 pairs	3 pairs	2 pairs	1 pair	None

Question 6

e4eeb   e4eeb

pla9d   plad9

br8dl   br8dl

c62h5   c62h5

A	B	C	D	E
All 4 pairs	3 pairs	2 pairs	1 pair	None

Question 7

6fswe	6fswe
jfu38	juf38
m8dh2	md8h2
co8ay	c08ay

A	B	C	D	E
All 4 pairs	3 pairs	2 pairs	1 pair	None

Question 8

ld9nv	ld9nv
3085j	3085j
djk48	dkj48
dl20f	dl20f

A	B	C	D	E
All 4 pairs	3 pairs	2 pairs	1 pair	None

Question 9

vv9dj	vv9dj
e8fmv	e8fmv
le03j	le03j
3mfk0	3mkf0

A	B	C	D	E
All 4 pairs	3 pairs	2 pairs	1 pair	None

Question 10

ofk4k	okf4k
fj893	ff883
dkc3b	dlpr4
mvmv9	mama9

A	B	C	D	E
All 4 pairs	3 pairs	2 pairs	1 pair	None

Question 11

9sn4f	9snff
19fj5	19fj5
fjqpw	fjjpw
mcpwj	mcppw

A	B	C	D	E
All 4 pairs	3 pairs	2 pairs	1 pair	None

Question 12

4e6mg	4emg6
fkd8a	fkda8
mv911	mv911
14fu7	14fu7

A	B	C	D	E
All 4 pairs	3 pairs	2 pairs	1 pair	None

Question 13

uwv90	uwv90
cui0a	cui0a
sdf87	sdf78
flp02	flp02

A	B	C	D	E
All 4 pairs	3 pairs	2 pairs	1 pair	None

Question 14

9cjfr	9cjjr
fk04f	kf000
gt48f	ggtt4
fp28f	fp82f

A	B	C	D	E
All 4 pairs	3 pairs	2 pairs	1 pair	None

Question 15

fbugf	fbugf
lpt8s	lpt8s
aprm6	aprm6
mwp84	mwp84

A	B	C	D	E
All 4 pairs	3 pairs	2 pairs	1 pair	None

Question 16

lpq93   lpq39
238f7   238f7
c9384   c9833
xlspe   xlspe

A	B	C	D	E
All 4 pairs	3 pairs	2 pairs	1 pair	None

Question 17

mvoe0   mvoe0
xzza8   xzza8
z3f95   zf395
cmdi4   cmdi4

A	B	C	D	E
All 4 pairs	3 pairs	2 pairs	1 pair	None

Question 18

6h98j   6h9j8
33611   36611
squak   squak
dd8nh   dd8hn

A	B	C	D	E
All 4 pairs	3 pairs	2 pairs	1 pair	None

Question 19

q35fy	q35fy
kf93h	kf39d
dj83p	dj83p
dhj4f	dhj4f

A	B	C	D	E
All 4 pairs	3 pairs	2 pairs	1 pair	None

Question 20

ee9lp	ee9ip
hel4p	h4lep
cmf83	cmf83
10385	10842

A	B	C	D	E
All 4 pairs	3 pairs	2 pairs	1 pair	None

Question 21

queen	queen
35985	35985
mcpwe	mcpwe
wr0pt	wr0pt

A	B	C	D	E
All 4 pairs	3 pairs	2 pairs	1 pair	None

Question 22

o0pla	o0pla
35gl9	35ggl
mci4p	mci4p
sssr5	ssrr5

A	B	C	D	E
All 4 pairs	3 pairs	2 pairs	1 pair	None

Question 23

gat93	gae39
vmb24	vmmbb
wpri3	wpri3
0248r	0428r

A	B	C	D	E
All 4 pairs	3 pairs	2 pairs	1 pair	None

Question 24

slwep	slwep
wpwpw	wppww
48fj5	48fj5
dm30c	dm30c

A	B	C	D	E
All 4 pairs	3 pairs	2 pairs	1 pair	None

Question 25

xui23	xui23
3p3i5	3p3i5
ept48	ept48
pi38s	pi38s

A	B	C	D	E
All 4 pairs	3 pairs	2 pairs	1 pair	None

Question 26

up8rd	uprd3
turni	tunri
foi38	foi38
0d09v	0d09v

A	B	C	D	E
All 4 pairs	3 pairs	2 pairs	1 pair	None

Question 27

cvm49	cvm94
dp297	dp297
wrpit	wrpit
24085	24085

A	B	C	D	E
All 4 pairs	3 pairs	2 pairs	1 pair	None

Question 28

3k5h6	k356h
dl40w	di205
s92mc	s922m
xm309	xm309

A	B	C	D	E
All 4 pairs	3 pairs	2 pairs	1 pair	None

Question 29

ls03u	ls03u
do28w	d028w
smcv4	smcv4
10846	10846

A	B	C	D	E
All 4 pairs	3 pairs	2 pairs	1 pair	None

Question 30

04l5j	04i5j
vn94p	vn94q
cmcpr	cmcpr
84563	84653

A	B	C	D	E
All 4 pairs	3 pairs	2 pairs	1 pair	None

ANSWERS TO SPEED AND ACCURACY

Q1. C, 2 pairs

Q2. A, all 4 pairs

Q3. D, 1 pair

Q4. B, 3 pairs

Q5. E, none

Q6. B, 3 pairs

Q7. D, 1 pair

Q8. B, 3 pairs

Q9. B, 3 pairs

Q10. E, none

Q11. D, 1 pair

Q12. C, 2 pairs

Q13. B, 3 pairs

Q14. E, none

Q15. A, all 4 pairs

Q16. C, 2 pairs

Q17. B, 3 pairs

Q18. D, 1 pair

Q19. B, 3 pairs

Q20. D, 1 pair

Q21. A, all 4 pairs

Q22. C, 2 pairs

Q23. D, 1 pair

Q24. B, 3 pairs

Q25. A, all 4 pairs

Q26. C, 2 pairs

Q27. B, 3 pairs

Q28. D, 1 pair

Q29. B, 3 pairs

Q30. D, 1 pair

Now move on to the next section of the guide.

CHAPTER 10

(FOLLOWING PROCEDURES)

ADMINISTRATIVE GRADE TESTS

The following procedures test is designed to test a candidate's ability to follow simple instructions and procedures. The test allows candidates to interpret and analyse the information provided in order to come to some conclusion.

For this section, you will be given 30 questions; 3 main questions with 10 sub questions. You will have multiple answers to choose from, some questions may require more than one answer.

We have deliberately provided you without a time frame in order for you to work through the questions carefully. You need to understand how these tests work and how to get to the correct answer. If you don't answer the questions correctly, you should take time to analyse your answers to understand where you went wrong.

Please circle the correct answer.

EXAMPLE

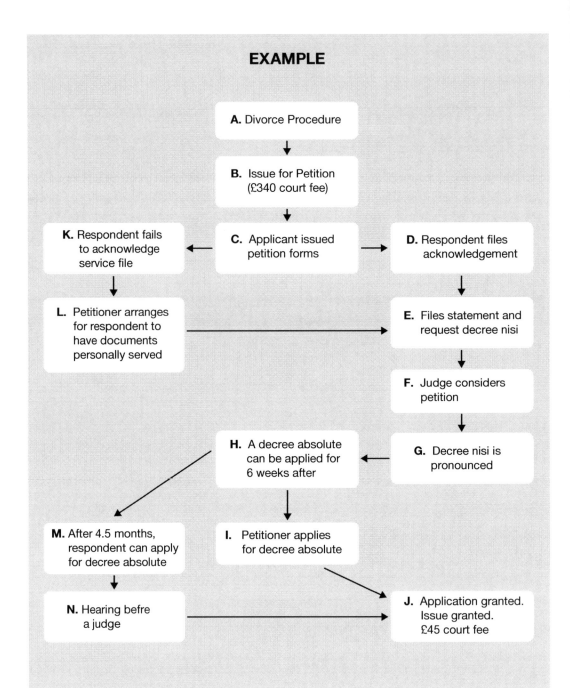

A. Divorce Procedure

B. Issue for Petition
(£340 court fee)

K. Respondent fails
to acknowledge
service file

C. Applicant issued
petition forms

D. Respondent files
acknowledgement

L. Petitioner arranges
for respondent to
have documents
personally served

E. Files statement and
request decree nisi

F. Judge considers
petition

H. A decree absolute
can be applied for
6 weeks after

G. Decree nisi is
pronounced

M. After 4.5 months,
respondent can apply
for decree absolute

I. Petitioner applies
for decree absolute

N. Hearing befre
a judge

J. Application granted.
Issue granted.
£45 court fee

Question

What is the next stage after a request has been made for decree nisi?

How to work it out

- You follow the diagram and work out which comes next in the proceedings.

Answer

F. Judge considers petition

FIGURE 1

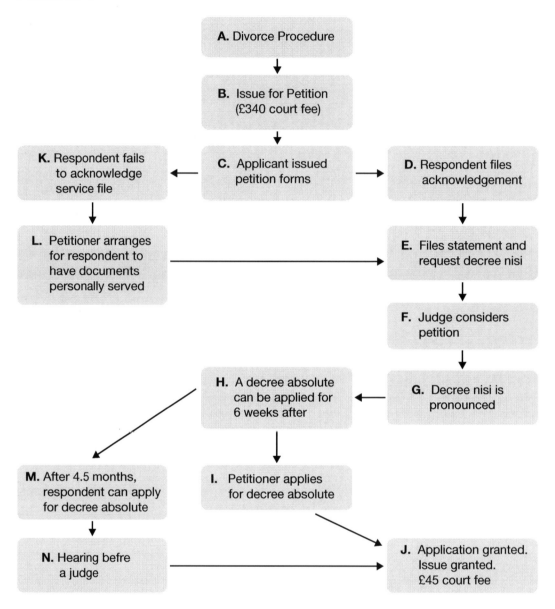

Question 1

Identify which stages could proceed after a decree nisi has been pronounced.

D	F	G	H	I	J	K	L	M	N

Question 2

Sandra has just filed acknowledgement of service in regards to her matrimonial order. What stage occurred just before this?

A	B	C	D	E	F	G	H	I	J

Question 3

A decree nisi has been pronounced. Millie wants to apply for a decree absolute as soon as possible. Assuming Millie applies six weeks after, what stages come next?

C	D	E	F	G	H	I	J	K	L

Question 4

At what stage(s) will there be court fees to pay?

B	C	D	E	F	G	H	I	J	K

Question 5

What stage(s) occur just before an application is granted?

D	F	G	H	I	J	K	L	M	N

Question 6

What happens when a respondent fails to acknowledge the service files?

D	F	G	H	I	J	K	L	M	N

Question 7

At what stage can a decree nisi be requested?

A	B	C	D	E	F	G	H	I	J

Question 8

What types of files can be applied for in the divorce proceedings?

A	B	C	D	E	F	G	H	I	J

Question 9

At what stage will you need a judge to determine whether or not your application has been successful?

D	F	G	H	I	J	K	L	M	N

Question 10

At what stage are the divorce statements filed for future reference?

A	B	C	D	E	F	G	H	I	J

FIGURE 2

Mr Walker, manager of a finance company is responsible for any dismissal or termination of employees. His managing assistant, David, and himself, are in charge of keeping records of employee's background, behaviour and any information deemed relevant in terms of the workplace. Mr Walker reports back to his director, Nathan Scott of any plausible situations that could require termination of an employment contract. Between them, they sit down once a month to discuss a person's records for possible cause to terminate their contract. They look at all the background evidence, information and knowledge to come to a reasonable conclusion as to whether or not that person deserves their contract to be terminated. It is Mr Walker who makes the final decision and implements any action required. The termination of an employee's contract is highlighted in the following requirements below:

The statutory notice required is:

- One week if the employee has been employed between one month and 2 years.
- One week for each completed year of employment. (Up to the maximum of 12 years).

Employers have the right to submit a summary dismissal in the case of gross misconduct and serious circumstances or crimes. Any relation to theft, assault, violence and fraud are all reasons enough to implement a summary dismissal. However, employers should investigate prior to such dismissals to ensure valid and solid reasoning for dismissal without notice.

Question 11

Whose responsibility is it to come to the ultimate decision as to whether or not a person's contract should be terminated?

A – David.
B – Mr Walker.
C – Nathan Scott.
D – All of them.
E – None of them.

Answer

Question 12

An employee has been accused of committing fraud. What should the employer's first action be? (TWO answers)

A – Implement summary for dismissal.
B – Issue a warning.
C – Gather up information in regards to the validity of the claim.
D – Ignore the problem – there is no evidence.
E – Talk about it in the monthly meetings.

Answer

Question 13

Which of the following pieces of information would most support the person's accusations?

A – If the accused denied committing fraud.
B – If sufficient evidence was collected to prove any fraud activity.
C – The accused handed in their resignation.
D – All of these.
E – None of these.

Answer

Question 14

Sam has been at the company for three weeks, but has some personal issues to deal with. He decides to resign. How many weeks of notice does Sam need to work?

A – One week.
B – Three weeks.
C – None.
D – Impossible to say.

Answer

Question 15

What would you expect the employers to do had they found out an employee was in court for assault?

A – Implement summary for dismissal.
B – Talk to the employee about it.
C – Keep it on record and wait to see what happens in court.
D – Ignore the problem.
E – None of these.

Answer

Question 16

Bill has been at the company for 18 years. He is coming up to retirement and wants to retire. How many weeks' notice does Bill have to work before leaving the company?

A – Three weeks.
B – Eighteen weeks.
C – Impossible to say.
D – None.

Answer

Question 17

Who does Mr Walker have to report to and give information about employee's performance and circumstances?

A – David.

B – Nathan Scott.

C – Bill.

D – None of these.

E – Impossible to say.

Answer

Question 18

Out of the following choices, what offence or serious misconduct is most likely cause for submitting a summary dismissal? (More than one answer can apply).

A – Laziness

B – Negligence

C – Aggressive behaviour

D – Swearing

E – Fraud

Answer

Question 19

Rachel has been the company's receptionist for over a year and a half. How long will Rachel have to work in terms of notice if she decided to resign?

A – One week.

B – Two weeks.

C – Eighteen weeks.

D – None.

E – Impossible to say.

Answer

Question 20

What should employers do before issuing a summary for dismissal?

A – Talk to the employee.

B – Talk to all the staff and get their opinion.

C – Collect all the information and evidence to support reasoning for dismissal.

D – Not let the employee know he/she is up for dismissal.

E – Go ahead and do it.

Answer

FIGURE 3

The law provides safety procedures and regulations that can be given to people who feel under threat or in possible danger. You can apply for a civil injunction or protection order if you feel under threat, harassed or intimidated. These injunctions last approximately 6 months and then have to be reviewed.

Many people feel it is necessary to apply for an injunction on a person. Injunctions are used as a safety procedure to ensure the safety and comfort of people and to offer protective measurements in regards to themselves, their families and their home.

Injunctions are provided on the basis of evidence and information to support your claim, which is required for an injunction to be made.

In the following passage, it gives two types of injunctions that could be implemented against a person.

You could file for either:

A **Non-Molestation Order** – prevents partners or ex partners from threatening violence or harm against you or your child. Any behaviour resulting in intimidation, harassment, stalking, violence can be seen as plausible causes to injunction a person.

An **Occupation order** – this order prevents a person from entering your home or living there. It regulates who lives in the family home to ensure safety for every person.

Under new legislation, breaching a non-molestation order is a criminal offence, which may come with the power of arrest.

Eligibility for applying for an injunction:

- You are or have been married to said person.
- You are or have been in a civil partnership with said person.
- You are or have been cohabitants with said person.
- You live or have lived in the same household.
- You are a relative of said person.
- You have a child together with said person.

Question 21

You want to stop someone from entering your home because of harassment issues. What protection order should you file for?

A – A non-molestation order.
B – An occupation order.
C – Not eligible for an injunction order.
D – Both.

Answer

Question 22

Out of the following, which of these incidents would least likely get an injunction?

A – Threatening violence to your ex-partner.
B – Stalking your child's school, until they come out.
C – Arguing with your husband.
D – Coming home to an abusive husband after he's been drinking.

Answer

Question 23

You are being threatened by your ex-partner. You have a child together. He turns up at your house in the middle of the night shouting and threatening. What reasons of eligibility for applying for an injunction are most appropriate? (TWO answers)

A – Being in a relationship.

B – You are a relative.

C – You have a child with said person.

D – You've never met the person before.

Answer

Question 24

In order to get an injunction, a law fee may apply. Who will have to pay the fee?

A – The applicant.

B – The accused.

C – The courts.

D – Impossible to say.

Answer

Question 25

What is an injunction for?

A – Stop people hassling other people.

B – To ensure safety of people by implementing procedures and regulations.

C – To arrest people who are displaying levels of misconduct and harassment.

D – All of the other

Answer

Question 26

Power of arrest occurs when…

A – An injunction has been made.

B – The victim drops the injunction order.

C – A breach of order takes place.

D – None of the above.

Answer

Question 27

Injunctions need… (TWO answers)

A – Lots of accusations against said person.

B – Cause of harassment, threats or violence against someone.

C – Evidence and support to back up the claim.

D – Police knowledge and background information to arrest someone.

Answer

Question 28

Out of the following, which of these incidents would most likely get an injunction?

A – Fighting with your partner

B – Heated argument with family resulting in some aggressive behaviour.

C – Your child saying your partner has been abusive.

D – Your partner denying any accusations been made about them.

Answer

Question 29

All non-molestation orders come with power of arrest.

A – True.

B – False.

C – Impossible to say.

Answer

Question 30

Injunction orders last for as long as that person needs it.

A – True.

B – False.

C – Impossible to say.

Answer

ANSWERS TO FOLLOWING PROCEDURES

Q1. H, I, J, M, N

Q2. C

Q3. I, J

Q4. B, J

Q5. I, N

Q6. L

Q7. E

Q8. E, H

Q9. N

Q10. E

Q11. B

EXPLANATION = although all the people mentioned in the statement have some role in terminating a person's contract, it is Mr Walker who makes the final decision.

Q12. C and E

EXPLANATION = the statement clearly indicates that monthly meetings are used to discuss any problem or concern in regards to employees so therefore this seems most logical. Considering it is an accusation, the employers need to follow up on anything that has been reported, therefore they should gather up information and evidence in relation to the situation.

Q13. B

EXPLANATION = finding evidence to support the accusation would prove most beneficial. If the employee were to hand in their resignation, this could be a sign of a guilty conscience, however this relies on a heavy assumption, so therefore would not be cause to support the accusation.

Q14. D

EXPLANATION = the statutory rights indicate that you need to work one week if you have been at the company between one month and two years. It does not indicate how long you would have to work had you only been there for three weeks, therefore it is impossible to say based on the information provided.

Q15. C

EXPLANATION = it would be most logical to file this on their record and keep track of what is happening in regards to their court case and the outcome. It would be least productive to question the employee about it, who is unlikely to tell you anything about it, nor would it be logical to ignore the problem. You do not have a solid reason to implement summary for dismissal due to the lack of knowledge or resources to go on.

Q16. C

EXPLANATION = the information provided does not mention anything about notice in regards to retirement. It also does not mention how many weeks would be needed to work for an employee that has been there eighteen years – "up to a maximum of 12 years", therefore it is impossible to say.

Q17. B

EXPLANATION = the statement clearly indicates that Mr Walker is to report back to the director, Nathan Scott.

Q18. C and E

EXPLANATION = aggressive behaviour and fraud are all reasonable forms of misconduct that could potentially lead to a summary dismissal. Behaviour and attitude that is hostile, aggressive and unlawful are all valid reasons for dismissal.

Q19. A

EXPLANATION = statutory rights indicate that employees need to work one weeks' notice if they have been employed at the company between one week and two years.

Q20. C

EXPLANATION = employers need valid and reasonable evidence and support to back up their reasoning for wanting to issue a summary for dismissal.

Q21. B

EXPLANATION = if you want to stop someone from harassing you and coming into your home, you are most likely going to file for an occupation order.

Q22. C

EXPLANATION = the statement provides clear and serious reasoning as to how a person can apply for an injunction. Arguing with someone does not give enough cause to file for an injunction.

Q23. A and C

EXPLANATION = eligibility criteria that applies under these circumstances is that the person was an ex-partner, and they have a child together.

Q24. D

EXPLANATION = it is impossible to say who pays any law fee. The statement and data provided does not mention anything about costing or legal fees, therefore it is impossible to indicate who would or would not pay for legal fees, if any.

Q25. B

EXPLANATION = although each statement has some logic in what it is saying, injunctions are primarily used to ensure safety and comfort for people who are experiencing behaviour of misconduct, harassment and/or violence from another person. Injunctions are not always used to arrest people and they do more than just stop people harassing, therefore the correct answer is B.

Q26. C

EXPLANATION = power of arrest happens when a breach of the order has occurred. For example, if said person was ordered not to contact the victim, and they do so, there is cause for power of arrest.

Q27. B and C

EXPLANATION = injunctions need to be filed in cause of behaviour that is said to be threatening, abusive or violent. Injunctions need to have as much evidence and support as possible to back up the reasoning for the injunction.

Q28. C

EXPLANATION = a child saying your partner has been abusive towards them is a solid reason for getting an injunction. Out of the choices, this example would most likely be a cause for concern and therefore is more likely to get an injunction.

Q29. B

EXPLANATION = the statement clearly indicates that "under new legislation, breaching a non-molestation order is a criminal offence, which may come with the power of arrest". The word 'MAY' is vital... it does not definitely come with this power and therefore not every molestation order will come with power of arrest.

Q30. B

EXPLANATION = injunction orders do not last for as long as a person needs it. In the statement, it illustrates a 6 month time scale and then has to be reviewed. This does not guarantee the injunction will be re-granted, so therefore this statement is false.

Now move on to the next section of the guide.

CHAPTER 11

MANAGERIAL TESTS

(Non-Fast Stream)

Applying for a managerial role within the Civil Service involves a different type of assessment as opposed to the testing used in previous chapters. Managerial positions have a great deal of responsibility, both to themselves and to other people. They need to be suitable to the job role and demonstrate great levels of managerial skills, knowledge and key leadership qualities.

The Non-Fast Stream Managerial Test uses three question types in order to assess one's abilities and skills. These question types include personality tests, attitudinal tests and situational awareness tests. Foremost, these tests are similar to personality tests which allow employers to engage with a person's character and personality traits. Personality, attitude and identity have become a significant influential factor in the job selection process and therefore it is important to be able to demonstrate high levels of skills, knowledge and attributes which are required.

As part of the Civil Service selection process, these assessments will help build up an overall depiction in regards to your individual and managerial style. Psychometric testing allows employers to identify valuable information by digging deeper into a person's persona and identifying key strengths and weaknesses. Such tests are designed to provide revelations which employers may otherwise have missed during the selection process.

Note: If you suffer with a disability or have a learning disability, please notify the department or agency prior to sitting the test. You will not be penalised, if anything, this will help you. Whether you need extra time, or need someone to read the questions etc, you won't receive this benefit if you do not notify them **prior** to the day of your test.

STRUCTURE OF THE TEST

The following questions will indicate the types of questions you will face in the Non-Fast Stream Managerial tests. So, it is important to carefully work through each question type and understand how to answer the questions. Your personality will be assessed through a series of question types. The test is very simple. It does not require any mathematical calculations or working out. You simply need to answer truthfully to provide a real sense of your characteristics and personality.

An important note to remember when undergoing such tests is to ensure that whilst you answer truthfully, you need to answer the questions in accordance with the job role. For this test, it is a position in a managerial role you are looking for. Therefore, you do not want to answer the questions based on your home life or how you act with friends and family. You need to answer the questions truthfully and professionally.

Please note that although there is no wrong or right answers for this chapter, in order to stand a chance of joining the Civil Service you need to answer the questions based on what they are looking for. Therefore we will provide you with explanations of what your answers might suggest to possible employers.

This chapter offers practice questions in relation to the following subject areas:

- **Personality Tests** – 40 questions
- **Attitudinal Tests** – 40 questions
- **Situational Awareness Tests** – 40 questions

We have not provided you with a time limit. This will allow you to work slowly and carefully throughout the chapter.

GENERAL TIPS FOR PASSING THE MANAGERIAL TESTS

- Whilst you need to answer this section with as much truth as possible, you need to consider what the Civil Service is looking for in relation to your answers.

- Carefully consider the phrasing of each statement. For example, a sentence starting with "I never" is powerful and assuming. The fact that you would never do something may give false pretences. You may have or would do something once and therefore 'never' would not apply.

- Read the statements carefully and make sure you understand what the question or statement is asking.

- Make sure you understand how to circle your answers. You do not want to be circling 5's if you strongly disagree. Make sure you know what each of the numbers represent.

- You want to show your personality and attitude as much as possible through your answers. Do not answer all the questions based on what you think is a good answer.

Good luck.

CHAPTER 12

PERSONALITY TESTS

MANAGERIAL TESTS

Personality tests are a form of psychometric testing and they are being used more during the selection process. Personality tests allow employers to look beyond experience and knowledge and gain insight into a person's character and personality. Such tests are designed to assess a person's individual and interpersonal behaviour based on attitude and behaviour.

For this test, you will be presented with a series of statements which you will answer either **strongly agree, agree, neutral, disagree or strongly disagree.** Try to ensure you answer the questions in a way that supports your application. Although having said this, you need to remain as truthful as possible. You do not want to respond to the test in a way that gives a false representation of yourself. So, be prepared to answer some of the questions that may not support your application.

Answer the questions as if you were already working for the Civil Service and ask yourself questions like 'would this be a good thing or bad?', 'is this relevant to working in the Civil Service?', 'is it appropriate?' and so on.

EXAMPLE

Question

I am a confident person.

Answer

How you answer the question is entirely on personal response. There is no right or wrong answer.

- If you answer **strongly agree,** this demonstrates extreme levels of confidence which might come across as egotistical, stubborn and domineering.
- If you answer **agree** you have good levels of confidence. You don't over embellish or come across as too assertive.
- If you answer **neutral,** you are not sure and haven't made up your mind.
- If you **disagree,** it means you lack confidence and have trouble expressing self-belief.
- If you **strongly disagree,** you have extreme levels of lacking self-confidence and therefore come across as shy, timid and introverted.

Circle the number that represents your chosen answer.

1	2	3	4	5
Strongly Disagree	Disagree	Neutral	Agree	Strongly Agree

Question 1

I have strong opinions and beliefs and I am not afraid to put them across.

1	2	3	4	5

Question 2

I have a direct approach in which I do things.

1	2	3	4	5

Question 3

I am not afraid to take charge of a task.

1	2	3	4	5

Question 4

I am willing to assist other people if they need my help.

1	2	3	4	5

Question 5

If I had to classify myself as either sensitive or insensitive, I would choose sensitivity.

1	2	3	4	5

Question 6

I prefer to do what I am told, as opposed to doing the telling.

Question 7

I would make the effort to get to know everyone I work with.

Question 8

I would consider myself authoritative.

Question 9

I am able to deal with difficult and stressful situations in a calm and poised manner.

Question 10

I am a confident person.

| 1 | 2 | 3 | 4 | 5 |

Question 11

I am able to manage a team of people effectively and successfully.

| 1 | 2 | 3 | 4 | 5 |

Question 12

I tend to take charge of a situation.

1	2	3	4	5

Question 13

I would consider myself a thick-skinned person.

1	2	3	4	5

Question 14

I am more of a practical person than a compassionate person.

1	2	3	4	5

Question 15

A career which I feel I could do well in, is much more important than a job with a higher salary.

1	2	3	4	5

Question 16

I am not able to compromise with other people.

1	2	3	4	5

Question 17

I would consider myself as an optimist as opposed to a fantasist.

1	2	3	4	5

Question 18

I like to lead a busy lifestyle.

1	2	3	4	5

Question 19

Some people would describe me as naïve.

1	2	3	4	5

Question 20

If I still had stuff to get done after finishing work; I would get it done at home.

1	2	3	4	5

Question 21

People say I am an extremely approachable person.

1	2	3	4	5

Question 22

I would describe myself as self-sufficient.

1	2	3	4	5

Question 23

I can handle a lot of information.

1	2	3	4	5

Question 24

Routine makes me feel comfortable and secure.

Question 25

It would be wrong to describe me as irresponsible and unreliable.

Question 26

My ability to work to a high standard would not be jeopardised if I had other people to mentor as well.

Question 27

I have a duty to myself and to my colleagues.

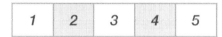

Question 28

I am highly driven to succeed.

Question 29

I have a clear direction of what I want from my career.

Question 30

Sometimes I get distracted with stuff going on in my personal life, that it occasionally affects my work.

1	2	3	4	5

Question 31

Before I say something, I often think to check whether it is the correct thing to say.

1	2	3	4	5

Question 32

I rarely let my emotions interfere with my work.

1	2	3	4	5

Question 33

I would consider myself a passionate person.

1	2	3	4	5

Question 34

I pay attention to small details.

1	2	3	4	5

Question 35

Given the chance, I would happily lead a group of people and set tasks for them.

1	2	3	4	5

Question 36

My job is in my top 5 of my list of priorities.

Question 37

I prefer to work in an environment where I don't have a great deal of responsibility.

Question 38

I get easily frustrated with people if they do something wrong.

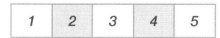

Question 39

I find it easy to think 'outside the box'.

Question 40

I consider myself an extremely impulsive person and often regret things after.

| 1 | 2 | 3 | 4 | 5 |

EXPLANATIONS TO PERSONALITY TESTS

Q1.

EXPLANATION = you should agree with this statement if you are the type of person who possesses strong views and opinions, and finds it difficult to bottle-up such feelings.

Q2.

EXPLANATION = if this is true about the way in which you work, you need to agree with the question. You have a firm, authoritative and direct approach, which demonstrates confidence and control.

Q3.

EXPLANATION = you should disagree if you do not like to be the centre of attention or take charge of a situation. Agree with the statement if you are comfortable with leading other people.

Q4.

EXPLANATION = if this is particularly true about yourself, you should agree to the statement. If you are the type of person who is willing to help other people it demonstrates your team skills and gregariousness.

Q5.

EXPLANATION = if you are a sensitive person, you need to agree with the statement. This is a question that could affect your outcome of your application. Managerial positions do not seek for sensitive people; for such roles people need to have grips of their emotional stability and show assertiveness and control.

Q6.

EXPLANATION = if you agree to this statement it shows that you prefer to be a 'follower' as opposed to a 'leader' and therefore could affect your managerial application. Managerial roles need to be leaders; leaders who can take charge and tell others what to do.

Q7.

EXPLANATION = if you are the type of person who comes across as friendly and sociable, then you would agree. You like to know the people around you, and therefore would provide a comfortable working atmosphere.

Q8.

EXPLANATION = if you are an authoritative, take charge, in control type person then you would agree. Managerial roles value assertiveness to ensure the work gets done and the person can demonstrate a firm, controlled and confident performance.

Q9.

EXPLANATION = you should disagree with this statement if you struggle to act in a calm and rationale manner when handling difficult tasks. Managerial roles expect a high level of composure, confidence and rationality when dealing with all types of situations.

Q10.

EXPLANATION = you should agree with this statement if you are able to show good levels of confidence and self-belief. Managerial roles need people who are able to show great levels of confidence and control and the ability to remain assured when dealing with situations and people.

Q11.

EXPLANATION = if this is true about yourself and you are able to effectively lead and manage a team of people, then you should agree to the statement. This is an extremely vital role in any managerial job, so stressing this personality trait may work in your favour.

Q12.

EXPLANATION = if you often find yourself taking charge and managing certain tasks, you should agree to the statement. It demonstrates your ability to quickly take charge of problems or situations and deal with them in an effective manner.

Q13.

EXPLANATION = if you show lack of sensitivity and have a tactless approach, you should agree with this statement. Thick-skinned suggests you show unresponsive and sometimes insensitive behaviour.

Q14.

EXPLANATION = if you believe you are more of a compassionate and sympathetic person as opposed to a person who is practical and gets on with every-day life, then you should disagree with this statement.

Q15.

EXPLANATION = if you're in the job for a large salary, you should disagree with this statement. You need to be truthful in regards to what you value the job as. Whether it is for self-accomplishment or if it's simply to pay the bills at home, answer honestly!

Q16.

EXPLANATION = if you struggle to compromise with other people and lack co-operation, then you must agree to this statement.

Q17.

EXPLANAITON = if you are optimistic and have a hopeful and confident approach, you should agree to this statement. However, if you feel as though you are often living in a dream world and are more of an idealist and wishful-thinker, you should disagree with the statement.

Q18.

EXPLANATION = if you enjoy always being on the go, working hard and having little time for relaxation, you must agree to the statement. People who prefer a more laid back lifestyle and are more carefree should disagree.

Q19.

EXPLANATION = if you are considered a naïve person, it might suggest you lack maturity and experience in regards to gaining a managerial position. You should carefully consider your answer for this question but answer truthfully, regardless of what it may say about you in terms of personality!

Q20.

EXPLANATION = if you're the type of person who, once finishes work believes they are done for the day then you should disagree. People who go that extra mile to finish their work find themselves taking their work home and continue working until its done should agree to this statement.

Q21.

EXPLANATION = managerial roles like people who are approachable in order for other employees to feel comfortable in the working environment. Employees who are afraid to come up to you and ask for your help or advice could jeopardise the company and more so, your role in a managerial position.

Q22.

EXPLANATION = if you're the type of person who needs guidance and structure from other workers then you should disagree. People who show the ability to work on their own initiative, independence and are confident in their own work should agree.

Q23.

EXPLANATION = managerial roles often require people who are able to handle lots of information at one time. People who struggle to do this may find the job more overwhelming than a person who is capable of dealing with lots of information.

Q24.

EXPLANATION = answering strongly agree to a question like this may suggest your inability for change. Answering strongly disagree might suggest that you are unable to stick to the rules and procedures of a company.

Q25.

EXPLANATION = if you are an extremely reliable and responsible person, then you should agree to the statement. However, if you often show signs of unreliability and struggle to deal with time limits and deadlines, you should consider your answer carefully.

Q26.

EXPLANATION = if you believe that you are capable of managing your workload as well as looking after and mentoring other employees, you should agree to the statement. If you think you would struggle to balance your own work load and helping other people, then you would need to disagree.

Q27.

EXPLANATION = this is an important asset to have in regards to any managerial position. Your ability to understand that you not only have a duty to yourself, but also to the others around you, proves valuable for a person who wants a career in a managerial position.

Q28.

EXPLANATION = if you are applying for a managerial role, it suggests that you have some level of desire to succeed. If this is true, you should agree to the statement. However, if you are not bothered about success in your career, then you need to answer honestly and disagree.

Q29.

EXPLANATION = if you are unsure or doubtful about what you want in terms of your career, you should answer honestly and disagree with the statement. If you are a person who knows exactly what you want and where your career is or should be heading, then you should agree.

Q30.

EXPLANATION = everyone gets distracted from time to time. It depends on how much you let it distract you and affect your work that is important. Managerial roles require a lot of focus and attention to detail, so it is important to answer the question truthfully.

Q31.

EXPLANATION = if you often find yourself pausing on something you were about to say, you should agree with the statement. If you are a person who often 'acts before they speak', you should consider disagreeing with the statement.

Q32.

EXPLANATION = if you struggle to keep your personal life and feelings from your work life, you should disagree. If you are the type of person who does not or rarely lets their emotions interfere with their workload, you should agree with the statement.

Q33.

EXPLANATION = if you have great levels of passion (in terms of your career) you should agree with the statement. If you do not have a great passion for your job then you should consider disagreeing with the statement.

Q34.

EXPLANATION = paying attention to the small details of a job is sometimes vital. Managerial roles sometimes require the ability to dig deeper into a problem or information and pick out the finer details. If you are able to do this you should agree with the statement.

Q35.

EXPLANATION = leading a group and setting tasks for other people is a fundamental job of a managerial role. It is your task to make sure everyone knows what they're doing, offer support when needed and lead the group effectively and successfully, if this is something you can do, you should agree.

Q36.

EXPLANATION = if your job does not make it onto your top 5 list of priorities, you should consider disagreeing with the statement. Managerial roles require a person who values their job a great deal and are able to show that they prioritise their job as a matter of importance.

Q37.

EXPLANATION = if this is particularly relevant to your belief, then you need to agree with the statement. Managerial roles however do require you to take great deals of responsibility and therefore your answer to this question proves significant.

Q38.

EXPLANATION = showing high levels of frustration might suggest you are overwhelmed and would struggle with the demands of the job. People who are able to express their frustration in a mature and helpful way are more likely to get a better result as opposed to a person who kicks off.

Q39.

EXPLANATION = some managerial work may require you to think on your feet and think 'outside the box'. In other words, you will need to show original thoughts and ideas and show creative and fast thinking. If you are the type of person who struggles to come up with new and original ideas, then you should disagree with the statement.

Q40.

EXPLANATION = acting on impulses can be seen as a positive and a negative. Acting on impulses demonstrates the ability to work on your own initiative and show the ability to act quickly if a situation requires you to do so. However, acting on impulses can sometimes lead to rash and problematic decisions, which could consequently affect the outcome.

CHAPTER 13

ATTITUDINAL TESTS

MANAGERIAL TESTS

Unlike personality tests, a negative response in an attitudinal test could result in the failure of your application. Attitudinal tests assess a candidate's ability to demonstrate the attitude which employers are looking for. If a candidate was unable to follow a simple instruction or follow the rules and procedures of the company, their application would be dismissed.

The use of attitudinal tests in relation to the Civil Service is to highlight a candidate's behaviour and attitude if they were to be employed. The test predicts how a candidate may act in a particular scenario and therefore it is important to establish their responses to ensure their application is successful.

The Civil Service selection process is used to filter out candidates who do not have the necessary skills or attitude to approach situations in a particular way. These tests are designed to test a candidate's responses in regards to important company procedures such as health and safety, equal opportunities, handling grievances and dismissals and the staff in which they will manage.

In this section, we have provided you with 40 practice questions so you can understand how to answer in accordance to what the Civil Service is searching for.

EXAMPLE

Question

I often make racist remarks.

Answer Choices

1 – Strongly disagree.
2 – Disagree.
3 – Neutral.
4 – Agree.
5 – Strongly agree.

Answer

- If your answer shows any indication of racial discrimination, this would be a likely cause to fail your application.
- Racial discrimination does not follow the equal opportunities policy in regards to the Civil Service and therefore would be reason enough to dismiss a person's application.

Circle the number that represents your chosen answer.

1	2	3	4	5
Strongly Disagree	Disagree	Neutral	Agree	Strongly Agree

Question 1

I believe that people aged 50 and over are incapable of change and not able to adjust to new ways of doing things.

Question 2

Everyone deserves the right to be treated as an equal at the workplace.

Question 3

I find it difficult to accept information from someone higher up than me when they are considerably younger than myself.

1	2	3	4	5

Question 4

My actions speak louder than my words.

Question 5

I believe that men are better at most jobs than women.

Question 6

I find it difficult to work with someone who I do not get on with.

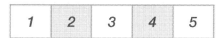

Question 7

It is sometimes okay to make an insulting and/or discourteous remark at work.

Question 8

I believe that it is important for everyone to follow the health and safety regulations of a workplace.

| 1 | 2 | 3 | 4 | 5 |

Question 9

If someone made a racist joke to the rest of the employees, I would ignore it.

| 1 | 2 | 3 | 4 | 5 |

Question 10

I think it's an invasion of privacy and morally wrong for companies to do random drug testing.

1	2	3	4	5

Question 11

I would not class taking pens and paper home for your personal use as stealing.

1	2	3	4	5

Question 12

What I do outside work, whether that be drugs or alcohol, is no concern of my employers.

1	2	3	4	5

Question 13

If you were late for work and nobody noticed, you would not tell anybody.

1	2	3	4	5

Question 14

If you knew someone was being sexually harassed at work, you would inform the authorities.

1	2	3	4	5

Question 15

If someone was being bullied at work, I would leave it up to them to sort it out.

1	2	3	4	5

Question 16

I find it hard to control my temper.

| 1 | 2 | 3 | 4 | 5 |

Question 17

Sometimes, an aggressive confrontation between two colleagues needs you to be equally aggressive to resolve the situation.

| 1 | 2 | 3 | 4 | 5 |

Question 18

I sometimes make the occasional joke relating to disabilities; only to people who are not disabled.

| 1 | 2 | 3 | 4 | 5 |

Question 19

I would feel offended if I reached out to shake someone's hand and they refused.

| 1 | 2 | 3 | 4 | 5 |

Question 20

I am unable to show sympathy to people who are grieving.

| 1 | 2 | 3 | 4 | 5 |

Question 21

I sometimes have a problem with people who are egotistical.

| 1 | 2 | 3 | 4 | 5 |

Question 22

I tend not to associate with people with strong religious beliefs.

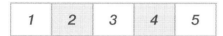

Question 23

In the event of the fire alarm going off at work, I like to be the person who jokes around and messes about.

Question 24

Becoming involved in listening to people's stories and problems will compromise your position.

Question 25

The only reason which I would not be disrespectful is that I wouldn't want someone to be disrespectful to me.

| 1 | 2 | 3 | 4 | 5 |

Question 26

I sometimes have mood swings that affects my relationships with the people I work with.

| 1 | 2 | 3 | 4 | 5 |

Question 27

If the floor was wet at work, but there was no sign to say 'warning', I would ignore it and leave it for the next person to sort.

Question 28

I tend to express my views without little thought for other people.

Question 29

You need to go to the toilet. You notice a person in a wheelchair is heading to the toilets also, you know you could quickly use the disabled toilet before they get there, so you go in.

Question 30

I would use a disabled car parking space at work so I don't have to walk far in the rain.

Question 31

You have employed two people to do the same job. Based on the fact that one is a woman and one is a man, you would offer different salaries.

Question 32

If I had two candidates who were equally as qualified as the other, but one was a National citizen and the other candidate was an immigrant, I am more likely to choose the candidate who is from this country.

Question 33

If someone upsets me, I always take it in my stride.

Question 34

If someone was rude to me, I would respond by retaliating in the same way.

Question 35

I believe sometimes you have to use abusive language in order to make a point.

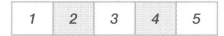

Question 36

If I was managing a team, I would give extra attention to those whom I found attractive.

| 1 | 2 | 3 | 4 | 5 |

Question 37

I work best when I am being told what to do.

| 1 | 2 | 3 | 4 | 5 |

Question 38

You hear a colleague teasing another member of staff about their sexuality. It is not your place to get involved.

| 1 | 2 | 3 | 4 | 5 |

Question 39

I would not find it slightly irritating nor would I be bothered if someone ignored my instructions.

| 1 | 2 | 3 | 4 | 5 |

Question 40

If I make a mistake, I usually can find someone else to blame.

| 1 | 2 | 3 | 4 | 5 |

EXPLANATIONS TO ATTITUDINAL TESTS

Q1.

EXPLANATION = believing that people over a certain age are unable to adapt and change to new ways of doing things is a sign of age discrimination, and therefore answering strongly agree could be grounds to fail your application.

Q2.

EXPLANATION = agreeing that everyone should be treated as an equal demonstrates your code of conduct and adhering to the equal opportunities policy and therefore is something employers would value.

Q3.

EXPLANATION = agreeing to this statement could also result in your application being rejected. You cannot be seen to be age discriminative. Just because someone is younger than you does not mean that they don't deserve a higher position.

Q4.

EXPLANATION = if your actions speak louder than your words, this might suggest that you struggle to express your views verbally. You take pride in putting your views across by acting upon it and this is not something the Civil Service wants to see in a managerial role.

Q5.

EXPLANATION = if you demonstrate in your answer that you agree that men are better at most jobs than women, this might indicate gender discrimination and therefore might affect your application in the Civil Service selection process.

Q6.

EXPLANATION = indicating that you struggle to work with people that you do not like or cannot get on with could affect your application. Managerial roles need people who, despite their differences, work alongside other people efficiently and comfortably to ensure maximum work ethic and potential.

Q7.

EXPLANATION = if you believe it is appropriate to make any rude or derisory remark at work then this could result in the failure of your application. Managerial roles need to act in a mature and experienced manner.

Q8.

EXPLANATION = agreeing to this statement means that you are considerate to the fact that health and safety regulations are there for a reason and therefore should be obeyed.

Q9.

EXPLANATION = if you ignored an act of racism, as somebody wanting a managerial role, your application would fail. Racist remarks, no matter how playful or 'joking around', need to be dealt with before a wider issue occurs.

Q10.

EXPLANATION = if you agree that random drug testing is wrong then this could have an impact on your application. Managerial roles need to be aware that anything relating to drugs needs to be handled in the upmost consideration and therefore drug tests are used to test people's safety at work.

Q11.

EXPLANATION = no employer would want a manager that believes taking pens and paper home for personal use is okay. It is not, it is a form of stealing. So agreeing to this statement could result in your application being rejected.

Q12.

EXPLANATION = employers have a duty to protect and look after their employees. Making sure their employees are not abusing alcohol or drugs is fundamental. Employers need to ensure a safe working environment for all their staff.

Q13.

EXPLANATION = a job in the Civil Service comes with great responsibility. You should be a person who can show integrity by owning up to late arrivals whether or not someone saw you.

Q14.

EXPLANATION = being oblivious and ignoring signs of sexual harassment could affect your application and result in a fail. Sexual harassment is a serious issue that needs to be addressed, therefore not coming forward is equally irresponsible.

Q15.

EXPLANATION = ignoring anti-social behaviour is irresponsible and unprofessional. As an aspiring manager, you will want to demonstrate commitment to your employees and ensure everyone's safety and equality is maintained.

Q16.

EXPLANATION = if you struggle to hold your temper, this shows lack of composure and control. As a person aspiring for a managerial role, you need to be fully prepared to deal with your emotions in a calm and collected manner; and not show aggressive behaviour in the workplace.

Q17.

EXPLANATION = believing that you can resolve a situation through aggressive behaviour and/or language is idiotic, immature and inexperienced. Situations need to be dealt with in a calm and rationale manner; getting aggressive will only make the situation more heated and more confrontational.

Q18.

EXPLANATION = making disabled jokes, despite whether or not a disabled person is present is a sign of disability discrimination. Whether they take it in their stride and are not affected by the joke; it is unacceptable behaviour in the workplace which managers need to address.

Q19.

EXPLANATION = as a person wanting a managerial position, you need to be able to show mature behaviour and not take things personally. Getting offended and irritated by someone not shaking your hand is pointless; you need to just take it in your stride and move on.

Q20.

EXPLANATION = the inability to show compassion and empathy towards someone in grievance does not show gregariousness or companionship. Managerial positions need to show comfort to those who are in need of it, without emotional integrity getting in the way.

Q21.

EXPLANATION = displaying high levels of issues with people who are egotistical shows your inability to work with different types of people. In every workplace, there are different types of people and personalities that you have to work with, and therefore creating problems will only make the matter worse.

Q22.

EXPLANATION = not associating with people based on someone's religion can be seen as discrimination. You may not agree with someone else beliefs or values, but everybody has different opinions and beliefs and therefore it would not be acceptable to base your judgements on someone, based on their religious ideologies.

Q23.

EXPLANATION = as a person applying for a managerial role you want to make sure that you display high levels of awareness and appreciation in relation to health and safety procedures. Messing about and joking around in the event of the fire alarm going off is immature and idiotic; traits that are undesirable as a manager.

Q24.

EXPLANATION = although engaging with people's personal problems should not really be brought to the workplace, sometimes it cannot be helped. Therefore as a manager, you want to be a person that employees feel comfortable talking to, in order to resolve any issues, concerns or problems they may have.

Q25.

EXPLANATION = answering agree or strongly agree to a question like this suggests your inability to look beyond what is being asked. There may be more than one reason as to why you wouldn't be disrespectful to someone, so if you have more than one reason (more than the reason given in the statement) then you should disagree.

Q26.

EXPLANATION = if this is true and you suffer with mood swings; this may affect your application into the Civil Service. As a manager, you should be able to control your mood and behaviour and set a good example for the rest of your team to follow.

Q27.

EXPLANATION = as an aspiring manager, you should deal with such problems quickly and effectively to ensure health and safety procedures are met. You do not want to be the reason as to why someone slips and falls, when you could have easily prevented the situation from happening.

Q28.

EXPLANATION = showing that you have little interest or concern of what other people think regarding something you have said or done shows lack of team effort. You need to be able to show that you not only think about yourself, but you also take into consideration other people's thoughts and feelings.

Q29.

EXPLANATION = using disabled toilets because the other toilets are occupied shows little concern of the needs of disabled people. If the disabled person was heading to the toilets, it shows lack of respect and courtesy.

Q30.

EXPLANATION = as a manager, you will be required to set a good example for the rest of your colleagues to follow. Using a disabled car parking space because it's closer to your workplace gives you no right. It shows lack of sensitivity and morals in regards to how this could affect other people.

Q31.

EXPLANATION = according to equal rights women and men should be paid equally for the same job. If you offered a man and a woman different pay, this illustrates gender discrimination and therefore could be a cause for your application to fail.

Q32.

EXPLANATION = choosing the national citizen candidate based on his nationality shows discrimination. If there was solid reasons to picking this candidate as opposed to the other one, that would be reasonable, but basing your decision purely on candidate's nationality is classed as discrimination.

Q33.

EXPLANATION = if you struggle to deal with criticism and fail to take it in your stride then this could affect your application. You do not want to come across as the type of person who is easily offended or upset. As a manager, you need to take the highroad and ignore remarks as opposed to retaliating.

Q34.

EXPLANATION = retaliating in a rude way because someone was rude to you, is no way of dealing with an issue. It would not resolve anything and would only make things worse in the long run. You should take it in your stride and ignore the rude remark.

Q35.

EXPLANATION = a manager should never use abusive language in order to get across a viewpoint. Managers need to be able to express their viewpoints without any heated or abusive language which would only indicate lack of professionalism.

Q36.

EXPLANATION = as a manager, you cannot be seen to delegate your time based on whom you find attractive. This is unprofessional and discriminates the other workers, therefore your answer may affect your application.

Q37.

EXPLANATION = if you work best when you are being told what to do as opposed to you doing the telling, a managerial role may not be for you. The role of a manager is to tell other team members their tasks and assignments and take control of the situation. It is not a job to sit back and let everyone do what they want.

Q38.

EXPLANATION = not getting involved when a situation requires you to tackle discrimination is unprofessional. As a manager, you would be expected to discourage such behaviour and remarks.

Q39.

EXPLANATION = as a manager, if someone doesn't follow your instructions or do as you have asked, you should respond and address the situation in order to get them to do what was previously asked.

Q40.

EXPLANATION = owning up to your mistakes and learning from your experience is a vital element in any job role. As a manager, you are there to set a good example, if you make a mistake and do not take the blame, it indicates your lack of compassion. It is important that people can own up to their mistakes, sooner rather than later.

CHAPTER 14

SITUATIONAL AWARENESS TESTS

MANAGERIAL TESTS

The Civil Service have to deal with lots of different and sometimes difficult situations. **Situational awareness tests** can be used during the selection process to assess a candidate's ability and understanding in regards to social situations. These tests are designed to evaluate candidate's responses as to how they would react in a particular situation.

These tests provide lots of different situations, all of which a civil servant could possibly face. Your job is to read through the passage and carefully rate the suggested responses in accordance to what seems the most appropriate or the most reasonable, or whether the response is less than acceptable.

The following 40 questions present a situation. Your task is to rank each response. You will be given four possible responses, and three ways to rate them. This means that you may rate two or more of the responses the same.

Note: if you believe two or more of the responses are reasonable and acceptable responses to make, you can rate these the same. If however, you believe that two or more suggested responses seem the **MOST** appropriate, you **DO NOT** rank any of the answers as the **MOST** appropriate, instead you would answer them both as 'acceptable'.

At the end of the chapter you will find the answers and explanations. Note that each question carries 4 marks – one mark for every correct response you answer. Make sure you take the time at the end of the chapter to look at where you went wrong. This will prove invaluable for future tests.

You have 3 rates to choose from for each suggested response:

- **A – Most appropriate response.**
- **B – An acceptable response.**
- **C – An unacceptable response.**

EXAMPLE

Situation

You notice that one of your colleagues is being sexually harassed. You know that the person has a record of doing this in the past. You have witnessed several incidents that would support this accusation. Touching, stalking and continuously emailing the 'victim'. The 'victim' is a good friend of yours and she opens up to you, but claims she doesn't want to take it any further.

Suggested Reponses:

1. Be there for your friend and calmly assure her that taking it further will help stop the sexual harassment.
2. Ignore everything you've seen and been told.
3. Follow the handbook procedures in relation to sexual harassment.
4. Go to the authorities yourself.

Rate:

A – Most **appropriate** response.
B – An **acceptable** response.
C – An **unacceptable** response.

Answer:

1	2	3	4
B	C	A	C

Response 1 is an acceptable response, which will offer your friend support in the situation. **Response 2** and **4** are less than acceptable because ignoring sexual harassment could be potentially dangerous and going to the authorities yourself goes against your friends wishes. **Response 3** is most appropriate because you will show the ability to follow the correct procedure in situations like this.

SITUATION 1

You notice that one of your colleagues is being threatened. You have witnessed several incidents that would support your accusation. You have heard the 'bully' claim 'he would smash up her house and everything in it'. You've seen him pin her to the wall, holding her around the neck and clinging on to the back of her hair. The 'victim' is a good friend of yours and she opens up to you, but claims she's tried to make him stop the threats and violence. She doesn't want to take it further because he "will make things even worse".

Suggested Responses:

1. Talk to the guy yourself. He might listen to someone else.
2. Tell your friend that she should consider telling someone higher up so they can enforce some safety procedure.
3. Ignore the situation. It's not your place to get involved.
4. Gather up possible choices for your friend and talk her through the options.

Rate the responses:

A – Most appropriate response.
B – An acceptable response.
C – An unacceptable response.

Answer:

1	2	3	4

SITUATION 2

A colleague complains to you that another member of staff is often making racist jokes. You have also noticed this on the rare occasion. You decided to overlook the matter previously because he was having family problems.

Suggested Responses:

1. You decide to ignore it again, he's obviously joking around.
2. You decide to bring it up as an issue in the next team meeting.
3. You talk to the colleague and explain that you will deal with it.
4. You quietly pull the member of staff aside and explain that his jokes are becoming an issue.

Rate the responses:

A – Most appropriate response.

B – An acceptable response.

C – An unacceptable response

Answer:

1	2	3	4

SITUATION 3

It is Monday morning and the cleaner for that shift is off on sick leave. It's 12:30 and you notice that on your way for your lunch break, the staff room is in a complete mess. The floor is wet and slippery, the bin is overflowing and there are several unwashed plates and cups left in the sink.

Suggested Responses:

1. Take your lunch break first and then give it a quick tidy after.
2. Do nothing. Somebody else probably has it already under control.
3. Inform whoever is in charge and report that there is a problem with the tidiness of the staff room.
4. You find a colleague who has just started and ask them to do you a favour and clean up the mess.

Rate the responses:

A – Most appropriate response.

B – An acceptable response.

C – An unacceptable response.

Answer:

1	2	3	4

SITUATION 4

You are on your lunch break. You head towards the staff room, but get stopped in your tracks by two people standing just around the corner arguing. They don't notice you, so you stand behind the corner. You overhear the conversation between two colleagues who you do not really know. The conversation seems to escalate and you overhear one of the colleagues blackmailing the other. Someone comes out of the staffroom and their conversation comes to an end. They walk in opposite directions.

Suggested Responses:

1. You decide to catch up with your colleague who was blackmailing the other and tell him you overheard everything and that you will report it.
2. Go to their manager and discuss what you have heard and let the manager deal with it accordingly.
3. Walk away and do nothing. You weren't meant to hear anything, so pretend that you didn't.
4. Follow the protocols that can be found in the staff handbook.

Rate the responses:

A – Most appropriate response.
B – An acceptable response.
C – An unacceptable response.

Answer:

1	2	3	4

SITUATION 5

You are in charge of looking over the bank statements for the month and to report back any feedback. You notice that numerous long-distant phone calls have all occurred between 11am and 1pm. These calls have been traced and made from the company's conference room. These phone calls are notably not for company use. You are unsure of who is making these calls.

Suggested Responses:

1. Bring it up in the next staff meeting and ask for a confession.
2. Report this phone activity to a member of management.
3. Wait and see if it happens again and then do something about it.
4. Be there between 11am and 1pm to see if anyone shows up and confront them.

Rate the responses:

A – Most appropriate response.
B – An acceptable response.
C – An unacceptable response.

Answer:

1	2	3	4

SITUATION 6

You have been working at the same place for over 2 years. You have always put in your best efforts to get the job done to the best of your ability. However, recent personal circumstances have made you lose focus at work. You are distracted, you're emotional, and you lack motivation.

Suggested Responses:

1. Talk to your manager directly about the situation and come up with a solution of how to deal with the problem.
2. Ignore the problem. I should be back to myself in no time.
3. Carry on with your work without telling anyone about your problem. You don't want to be a burden.
4. Tell someone you work with and maybe they can help you.

Rate the responses:

A – Most appropriate response.
B – An acceptable response.
C – An unacceptable response.

Answer:

1	2	3	4

SITUATION 7

You are on your way to work. Up ahead you notice a lot of traffic. You get stuck in traffic for 30 minutes. You are listening to the radio traffic updates and realise that you are stuck in traffic because of a car collision. There is no way of turning back or changing direction, so you have to sit and wait for the traffic to start moving. You are unsure about what time that will be.

Suggested Responses:

1. Wait until you know what time you will arrive at work before phoning in late.
2. Just turn up to work late without phoning in before with a reason as to why you arrived late.
3. Keep your manager regularly updated on your whereabouts and your expected time of arrival.
4. Phone your team leader and tell them about why you will be late.

Rate the responses:

A – Most appropriate response.
B – An acceptable response.
C – An unacceptable response.

Answer:

1	2	3	4

SITUATION 8

You are assigned a creative new project with another co-worker. He has been working in the same department for 10 years longer than you. You notice that he is not putting much effort into the project nor giving you any ideas to the project.

Suggested Responses:

1. Carry on with the project as best you can and then let him take half the credit at the end.
2. Notify your leader about the lack of participation of your co-worker and carry on with the project.
3. Speak to your co-worker about his lack of effort and participation and ask him politely to take the project more seriously.
4. Speak with your co-worker and tell him you quit because you are not doing the project by yourself anymore.

Rate the responses:

A – Most appropriate response.
B – An acceptable response.
C – An unacceptable response.

Answer:

1	2	3	4

SITUATION 9

You have been promoted to a team leader. You have thought of a creative new idea that you believe could improve your work progress. You talk to a few colleagues and some agree with your idea and some do not.

Suggested responses:

1. You ask your manager to conduct a presentation about your idea so you can voice your opinion.
2. You do not take your idea any further because it may spark some conflict with the people who disagreed with the idea.
3. You put your idea into action without discussing it with anyone.
4. You put together a portfolio of all your ideas and try to convince everyone that your idea is strong and beneficial.

Rate the responses:

A – Most appropriate response.
B – An acceptable response.
C – An unacceptable response.

Answer:

1	2	3	4

SITUATION 10

You are in charge of a team. You notice that one of the employees is continuously late. You have pulled him aside before to address the situation and he assured you that it would not happen again, but he continues to turn up late by approximately 20 minutes each time.

Suggested responses:

1. Notify that he will have to make up the time each time he is late.
2. Give him another chance and warn him if his lateness continues, further action will be taken.
3. Discuss his working hours, and try to find a way of allowing him to start later and finish later.
4. Issue a formal warning advising that he should improve his time keeping skills or further action will be taken.

Rate the responses:

A – Most appropriate response.
B – An acceptable response.
C – An unacceptable response.

Answer:

1	2	3	4

SITUATION 11

You are just about to finish a busy shift. Your colleague who is meant to replace you for the next shift has phoned in and said she will be half an hour or so late. You had made dinner plans with your partner and wanted to leave on time.

Suggested responses:

1. Finish your shift and leave anyway. It's not your responsibility.
2. Phone up your partner and tell them you are going to be late.

3. Tell one of the colleagues who is beginning their shift to notify the employee who is going to be late of any updates and information they need to know and then leave at the end of your shift.

4. Continue working and then wait for the late employee to arrive and explain you are upset and that you had made plans.

Rate the responses:

A – Most appropriate response.

B – An acceptable response.

C – An unacceptable response.

Answer:

1	2	3	4

SITUATION 12

The Civil Service is renowned for its vital role it plays in the Government. Civil servants serve the Government who is in action. You took the job on the basis that you would be serving Government views as opposed to views from political parties. Recently, you feel as though you are becoming too involved in political assertions.

Suggested responses:

1. Ask other colleagues if they feel the same and then discuss what to do next.

2. Take your concerns straight to your manager and discuss your concerns.

3. Refuse to do your work based on political principles and justifying your position by claiming that engaging in political views of parties was not in the job description.

4. 'Leak' the confidential and political views of what is being enclosed to other sources.

Rate the responses:

A – Most appropriate response.
B – An acceptable response.
C – An unacceptable response.

Answer:

1	2	3	4

SITUATION 13

You are the supervisor of the department. One of your employees complains to you that he is feeling overwhelmed in his job. He has only been in the position for 6 months and is still on a probationary period. He claims that he feels apprehensive and lacks self-confidence in regards to the work he should be doing.

Suggested responses:

1. Offer advice and support in regards to his job role and responsibilities. Tell him he can come to speak to you anytime.
2. Go to the manager and let him deal with it.
3. Tell him to get on with his job without complaining.
4. Tell him that considering he is still on a probationary period, you are going to let him go if he feels too incompetent for the job role.

Rate the responses:

A – Most appropriate response.
B – An acceptable response.
C – An unacceptable response.

Answer:

1	2	3	4

SITUATION 14

A co-worker is undermining you. You have noticed on several occasions that your co-worker often dismisses your opinions and ideas, he doesn't follow your orders and tells colleagues sly and unprofessional jokes about you.

Suggested responses:

1. Rise above it and ignore your co-worker and his antagonistic behaviour.
2. Raise the problem with your co-worker and use hostile and somewhat aggressive language to get your point across.
3. Read through the staff handbook to see what you can do about the problem.
4. Raise the issue with your supervisor/manager and get them to sort the problem out.

Rate the responses:

A – Most appropriate response.
B – An acceptable response.
C – An unacceptable response.

Answer:

1	2	3	4

SITUATION 15

You have an important meeting in one hour. You realise you have left your notes and documents at home. If you left now you know you will be at least 15 minutes late for the meeting.

Suggested responses:

1. Go home and quickly get the documents. You won't be able to do the meeting without them.
2. Reschedule the meeting.

3. Go into the meeting and try to remember what the important information was you had written down.
4. You have an hour. Use that time to quickly make some new notes and memorise those instead.

Rate the responses:

A – Most appropriate response.
B – An acceptable response.
C – An unacceptable response.

Answer:

1	2	3	4

SITUATION 16

You receive a phone call at work saying that you need to collect your child from school because she has been really sick. You cannot find your supervisor anywhere, so you leave without finding them.

Suggested responses:

1. Tell a co-worker and get them to inform management of your situation.
2. Leave without telling anyone, you might be back before management realises.
3. Call your manager and explain your situation. If you get their voicemail, leave a message.
4. Wait until you get back and speak to your manager.

Rate the responses:

A – Most appropriate response.
B – An acceptable response.
C – An unacceptable response.

Answer:

1	2	3	4

SITUATION 17

You have recently noticed that one of your co-workers has been struggling to deliver their work on time. There is no obvious reason for the lateness of his work. You have also noticed that the work he does eventually get in seems to have quite a few mistakes.

Suggested responses:

1. Talk to your team manager on their behalf and tell them you are concerned with your colleagues work. Allow your manager to deal with the issue in a professional way.
2. Speak to other members of the team and see if they have noticed the same problem.
3. Bring up the issue in the next staff meeting.
4. Speak with your co-worker and ask them if they are ok, and they you have noticed them struggling. Offer to help them if they need it.

Rate the responses:

A – Most appropriate response.
B – An acceptable response.
C – An unacceptable response.

Answer:

1	2	3	4

SITUATION 18

An important presentation is taking place at the end of the day. You are working on your manager's presentation to make some final technical adjustments. You open up an email and you realise it is a virus. You realise that the presentation has disappeared. It's all gone.

Suggested responses:

1. Inform your supervisor that one of your co-workers lost all the work.
2. Own up to your mistake and inform your manager immediately.
3. Wait until the time of the presentation and then confess.
4. Do not tell your manager, it's his presentation.

Rate the responses:

A – Most appropriate response.
B – An acceptable response.
C – An unacceptable response.

Answer:

1	2	3	4

SITUATION 19

You have noticed that two colleagues who use to work well together are 'at each other's heads'. They blame each other for the slightest thing and refuse to work in a team together.

Suggested responses:

1. Address every person in your team and explain the protocol of expectations and requirements as employees.
2. Pull the two colleagues aside and explain your concerns and that they need to address their issues professionally.

3. Ignore the problem, they will sort it out eventually.
4. Ask another colleague to monitor their behaviour.

Rate the responses:

A – Most appropriate response.
B – An acceptable response.
C – An unacceptable response.

Answer:

1	2	3	4

SITUATION 20

Leaving valuable property in the drawers of your desk is discouraged. Staff are told when employed that the company cannot accept any loss or damage or personal property if left unattended. You left your mobile in the drawer of your desk and it's now missing. The next day a colleague comes in with a new phone, identical to the one that went missing.

Suggested responses:

1. Create a heated argument with your colleague and demand he gives you the phone.
2. Go to management and explain what's happened and get them to demand back the phone.
3. Ask management to look at CCTV in order to establish if the colleague went near your desk and into your drawers.
4. Wait until your colleague leaves his phone unattended and check it to see if it was yours.

Rate the responses:

A – Most appropriate response.
B – An acceptable response.
C – An unacceptable response.

Answer:

1	2	3	4

SITUATION 21

You are feeling really unwell at work today. You've been sick a couple of times but you decided to stay until the end.

Suggested responses:

1. You do not tell anyone that you are feeling ill. You don't want to be a burden.
2. You inform your supervisor that you are not feeling well and may have to leave if you get worse.
3. You tell your supervisor that you are not feeling well but will try and carry on until the end of the day, but you might not be feeling well enough to come into work tomorrow.
4. You realise you can't make it till the end of the day and decide to go home.

Rate the responses:

A – Most appropriate response.
B – An acceptable response.
C – An unacceptable response.

Answer:

1	2	3	4

SITUATION 22

It's Sunday night and you are having a party. You weren't going to drink because you knew you had work in the morning. Everyone was drinking and you ended up drinking and getting really drunk.

Suggested responses:

1. Phone in work the next morning and say you are unable to make it into work.
2. Go into work and do as least amount of work as possible.
3. Drink lots of water at work and continue on with work.
4. Tell your manager that you are hung over and need to take your lunch break early.

Rate the responses:

A – Most appropriate response.
B – An acceptable response.
C – An unacceptable response.

Answer:

1	2	3	4

SITUATION 23

You overhear a colleague harassing a new employee. The company has strict rules and procedures in place to tackle harassment in the workforce. The colleague has been at the company for a long time and is the brother of the manager.

Suggested responses:

1. Confront your colleague and warn him against harassing other employees.
2. Tell the new employee about the harassment rules and procedures in place.

3. Go to the manager and explain the harassment situation, despite the colleague being related to the manager.
4. Go to your team leader and tell them what you have witnessed.

Rate the responses:

A – Most appropriate response.
B – An acceptable response.
C – An unacceptable response.

Answer:

1	2	3	4

SITUATION 24

You overhear a conversation on your lunch break. Two of your colleagues are talking about the new employee in an extremely sexual manner. Nobody else, apart from you and the two colleagues hear the conversation.

Suggested responses:

1. Ignore the conversation if you are 100% nobody else heard it.
2. Pull them aside and politely ask them not to sexualise other employees.
3. Bring up the incident in a staff meeting and use this incident as an example of sexual discrimination.
4. Tell the new employee that she is being sexualised and deal with the problem.

Rate the responses:

A – Most appropriate response.
B – An acceptable response.
C – An unacceptable response.

Answer:

1	2	3	4

SITUATION 25

You realise that one of your colleagues has accepted a free gift from a third party. Company rules strictly imply that no employee is to accept any gift of any kind in relation to their job. The colleague offers you to accompany them on the trip that was given to them.

Suggested response:

1. You kindly accept the offer.
2. You recommend that your colleague should return the tickets.
3. Turn down the offer and ignore the situation.
4. Tell your supervisor/manager of this incident.

Rate the responses:

A – Most appropriate response.
B – An acceptable response.
C – An unacceptable response.

Answer:

1	2	3	4

SITUATION 26

You and a colleague are co-operating on a project given by your supervisor. You notice that your colleague is missing agreed deadlines because he has an increased regular workload. Your performance report is due at the beginning of next week.

Suggested responses:

1. Help your colleague with his extra workload and then get on with your project.
2. Tell your supervisor that you may miss the deadline because of your colleague's inability to stick to deadlines.
3. Ask your supervisor for an extension.
4. Tell your colleague that you are concerned with his timekeeping skills and that they need to focus in order to get the job done on time.

Rate the responses:

A – Most appropriate response.
B – An acceptable response.
C – An unacceptable response.

Answer:

1	2	3	4

SITUATION 27

Your supervisor selects you to represent the company's new proposition. You will head negotiations with representatives and take charge of the presentations. Your supervisor tags along for the first two presentations and you notice that he seems to undermine everything you say or do, resulting in you feeling undermined and self-conscious.

Suggested responses:

1. Assert yourself more in the presentation to make sure you are heard over your supervisor.
2. Plan to talk to your supervisor before the next meeting.
3. Refuse to work alongside your supervisor in these presentations.
4. Pull your supervisor aside in the break and explain to him your feelings and the impact of his behaviour.

Rate the responses:

A – Most appropriate response.
B – An acceptable response.
C – An unacceptable response.

Answer:

1	2	3	4

SITUATION 28

Rumour goes around your workplace indicating that you are looking for another job. The rumour is true, and you want a job where you can fully utilise your skills and knowledge. However, you haven't told anyone at work that you are looking at other jobs.

Suggested responses:

1. Admit to the rumours and explain that you are looking for another job.
2. They're just rumours at the moment, so ignore the rumours and wait until you know for sure.
3. Tell your current employers that you are thinking of leaving.
4. Lie to your colleagues and say you're not planning to leave.

Rate the responses:

A – Most appropriate response.

B – An acceptable response.

C – An unacceptable response.

Answer:

1	2	3	4

SITUATION 29

You have no one to watch your child. Your babysitter phoned and said she was sick, your husband has gone to work, and the rest of your family and friends are either at work or have made other commitments. You have work in an hour.

Suggested responses:

1. Don't go into work; your child is your main priority.
2. Show up to work with your child and hope your supervisor doesn't notice.
3. Phone your supervisor and explain your situation and that you are trying to make arrangements before you're meant to start work.
4. Take your child to work before you're due to start work and explain to your supervisor your predicament.

Rate the responses:

A – Most appropriate response.

B – An acceptable response.

C – An unacceptable response.

Answer:

1	2	3	4

SITUATION 30

You have been notified about a possible promotion that is up for grabs. You are unsure whether you should apply.

Suggested responses:

1. Apply for the promotion. You have nothing to lose.
2. Speak to your supervisor and ask for their advice.
3. Hold back on applying until you have made an informed decision.
4. Weigh up your options and determine whether you are cut out for the job.

Rate the responses:

A – Most appropriate response.
B – An acceptable response.
C – An unacceptable response.

Answer:

1	2	3	4

SITUATION 31

You are the supervisor of the department. One of your colleagues has come to you for advice. He's been at the company for only a year and a half and is considering applying for an executive position. You've worked closely with this colleague and you've noticed he is extremely shy and lacks self-confidence and hasn't fully grasped the knowledge and expertise for an executive role.

Suggested responses:

1. Tell him that he doesn't 'have it' for the role of an executive.
2. Politely indicate both his strengths and weaknesses and advise him to consider waiting until he is more qualified.

3. Tell him to apply for it even though you know he won't get it and will affect his confidence levels even more.

4. Tell him not to go for it. Your best friend is going for it and won't stand a chance.

Rate the responses:

A – Most appropriate response.

B – An acceptable response.

C – An unacceptable response.

Answer:

1	2	3	4

SITUATION 32

You are conducting an induction for three new employees, all of which will be working in the same department as you. You learn that one of the new employees has a heart condition called HCM (hypertrophic cardiomyopathy). She claims that she may experience shortness of breath, exercise intolerance and chest pain, all symptoms of her cardiac disease.

Suggested responses:

1. Explain to her had you known this before employing her you would not have given her the job because you need someone whose work isn't going to be affected.

2. Ask her if there are any requirements she needs in order to make her more comfortable and anything she needs to accommodate her health, to let you know.

3. Explain that you are extremely concerned with her health in regards to performing this stressful job role.

4. Tell her that you are fully committed to equal opportunities and she will not be treated any different to other members of staff.

Rate the responses:

A – Most appropriate response.
B – An acceptable response.
C – An unacceptable response.

Answer:

1	2	3	4

SITUATION 33

You are the project leader for four team members. Your task is to make sure no problems arise from the project that they are co-ordinating on. Two of the members tell you that they won't be able to make the project deadlines. You know that if the deadlines are not met, you will be in trouble with the managing director.

Suggested responses:

1. Discuss with the two members the reasons why they are unable to meet the deadlines, evaluate the remains of the project left to do and create an action plan in order to finish the project.
2. Give the other two members more work to make sure the work gets done on time.
3. Advise them that if they don't get the project done on time, there will be consequences.
4. Go straight to the managing director and ask for an extension on their initial deadline.

Rate the responses:

A – Most appropriate response.
B – An acceptable response.
C – An unacceptable response.

Answer:

1	2	3	4

SITUATION 34

You are the leader of a large group of 18 employees. They are all working on the same project. You notice that they have all been playing an active role, except one. A shy, self-conscious employee who struggles to voice their opinion. You want to make sure that everyone plays an equal part in this project.

Suggested responses:

1. Tell the employee to quit being childish and get involved.
2. Quietly speak to the employee and tell them that you have noticed an issue and try to come up with a solution.
3. Offer advice and support subtly to the employee and encourage them to take more of an active role.
4. Tell the employee that you are unhappy with his work ethic during this project, and that you want to continue the project without him.

Rate the responses:

A – Most appropriate response.
B – An acceptable response.
C – An unacceptable response.

Answer:

1	2	3	4

SITUATION 35

You have been sent an email from a senior manager from the department you are about to join in 2 months' time. The senior manager stresses in the email that you will be joining their department at the busiest time, and that you should be fully prepared to make this transition into your new job role. Your current supervisor advises that you do your utmost to ensure a smooth transition. You have never worked in that type of role before.

Suggested responses:

1. Research on the internet about the job role you are about to go into and write down key notes.
2. Email the senior manager and ask if you could have a one-to-one meeting to find out all the information you will need to know before starting your new job.
3. Email the senior manager back thanking her for the email and that you look forward to seeing her in a couple of months.
4. Email the senior manager and ask whether she can give you any advice or feedback about what you may be working on when you start your new job.

Rate the responses:

A – Most appropriate response.
B – An acceptable response.
C – An unacceptable response.

Answer:

1	2	3	4

SITUATION 36

The peak business period for the year is fast approaching and you need to manage a team of six people. Your team is undoubtedly feeling the pressure and strain. So much so, that their work is being affected and errors are being made. Your team tells you that they are unsure and confused about what it is that they are meant to be doing.

Suggested responses:

1. Sit down with your team in regular meetings and go through the objectives and goals, make sure everyone knows what they are doing and how they are getting on.
2. Inform your team that you do not care for the careless work that they are doing and that things need to improve.
3. Establish goals and objectives for the projects and give them to each team member and explain what they should be doing.
4. Ignore the problem; your team are stressed out, but they will adapt to the pressures of the job and improve their work.

Rate the responses:

A – Most appropriate response.
B – An acceptable response.
C – An unacceptable response.

Answer:

1	2	3	4

SITUATION 37

You have recently been appointed supervisor of the department. You did not realise how much your workload would increase. You are feeling stressed and disorganised and unprepared.

Suggested responses:

1. Tell the head of the department that you weren't aware of the workload of the job and that you are not qualified to take on such a substantial role.
2. Form action plans and objectives, and organise your work so that you are fully prepared and know what to do and when to do it by.

3. Speak with your head of the department and ask them for any advice or support that they could offer.

4. Get on with the job. You will soon adapt to your new role as supervisor.

Rate the responses:

A – Most appropriate response.

B – An acceptable response.

C – An unacceptable response.

Answer:

1	2	3	4

SITUATION 38

You have noticed one of your colleagues continuously turning up to work with a hangover. You let it go a few times because it wasn't a big deal. The situation is becoming more frequent. You've noticed silly mistakes in their work and that it takes them longer to complete a task.

Suggested responses:

1. Ask your other colleagues if they have noticed the same problem and decide what action to take.

2. Bring up the issue in the next staff meeting, addressing the issue there will guarantee the situation will get sorted.

3. Directly speak with the employee and tell them you have noticed his hangovers and try to come to some agreement.

4. Speak to your supervisor and tell them you have noticed unprofessional behaviour from an employee which should be dealt with.

Rate the responses:

A – Most appropriate response.
B – An acceptable response.
C – An unacceptable response.

Answer:

1	2	3	4

SITUATION 39

You have an important doctor's consultation that can only be scheduled half way through your lunch break. You know if you go you are going to be late back to work.

Suggested responses:

1. Go anyway and hope that you make it back in time before anyone realises that you were late.
2. Go to your doctor's appointment and don't return back to work for the day.
3. Find your supervisor and explain to them your situation and that it is an urgent appointment that can only be scheduled around this time.
4. Tell your supervisor and ask them if you can make up the time at the end of the day.

Rate the responses:

A – Most appropriate response.
B – An acceptable response.
C – An unacceptable response.

Answer:

1	2	3	4

SITUATION 40

It's your Christmas party at work. You failed to finish a project on time, which should have been sent off before the end of the day. You only had a couple more pages to write.

Suggested responses:

1. Enjoy the party with everyone, and worry about the project later.
2. Quickly finish the project, and then return to the party.
3. Explain to your co-worker that you are worried about the project.
4. Tell yourself that it is too late to do anything about it.

Rate the responses:

A – Most appropriate response.
B – An acceptable response.
C – An unacceptable response.

Answer:

1	2	3	4

ANSWERS TO SITUATIONAL AWARENESS TESTS

Q1. 1 = C, 2 = B, 3 = C, 4 = B

EXPLANATION = Reponses 1 and 3 would prove irresponsible, unresponsive and least appropriate. You cannot ignore a matter of threatening behaviour nor can you take matters into your own hands. Response 2 and 4 are reasonably acceptable. It demonstrates your initiative to try and aid your friend calmly and supportively, without looking too pushy or demanding.

Q2. 1 = C, 2 = C, 3 = B, 4 = A

EXPLANATION = Response 1 demonstrates your inability to follow up on a cause for concern, particularly when you have noticed it also. Response 2 seems a little insensitive to bring up an issue in front of everyone. Response 3 allows your colleague to understand that you will deal with it and gives you time to form some action plan. Response 4 is the most appropriate because it directly solves the issue with the member of staff in a polite, sensitive and calm manner.

Q3. 1 = C, 2 = C, 3 = A, 4 = C

EXPLANATION = Response 1 means that you will be late back to work, so would therefore not be an acceptable response. Response 2 relies on a heavy assumption that it's already being taken care of. This may not be the case and needs to be reported. Response 3 is the most appropriate. You need to let whoever is in charge aware of the problem, so that they can deal with it quickly and effectively. Response 4 shows lack of respect towards new employees and they shouldn't feel trapped in cleaning up just because they are the new employee.

Q4. 1 = C, 2 = B, 3 = C, 4 = A

EXPLANATION = it would be irresponsible to take matters into your own hands (Response 1), which could put you and your other colleagues in danger. Response 2 is an acceptable response as it will give members of management the chance to act. Response 3 is unacceptable because it would be irresponsible to sit back and do nothing. Response 4 is the most appropriate because you will be following the process of how to handle such situations in the correct and laid out manner.

Q5. 1 = C, 2 = A, 3 = C, 4 = C

EXPLANATION = Response 1 would be impractical because no one will confess publically, the situation should be dealt with covertly. Response 2 is the most appropriate response, it allows management to decide how to go about handling the situation. Response 3 is irresponsible, the employee has made numerous long-distance phone calls which should be addressed as quickly as possible. Response 4 means that you would be taking matters into your own hands, but it is not your place to do so; your job is to 'report back any feedback'.

Q6. 1 = A, 2 = C, 3 = C, 4 = B

EXPLANATION = Response 1 would be the most appropriate response. It would allow you to deal with the problem directly and quickly and make your manager aware of your personal problems. Response 2 and 3 would be ineffective. Not dealing with the matter or not telling anyone could jeopardise your job role. You should speak to someone and make them aware of your situation. Response 4 is an acceptable response because it will allow you to talk to someone and get some help from a friendly face at work.

Q7. 1 = C, 2 = C, 3 = A, 4 = B

EXPLANATION = Response 1 would be ineffective and irresponsible. You should phone in late when you first know that you are going to be late. Response 2 is also ineffective. You should always let your manager/team leader know if you are going to be late. Response 3 is the most effective response. Keeping your manager regularly updated on your whereabouts will keep them fully aware of the situation. Response 4 is an acceptable response. Phoning your team leader will ensure that they will know that you are going to be late.

Q8. 1 = C. 2 = B, 3 =A, 4 = C

EXPLANATION = Response 1 would be ineffective. You should not be made to do all the work in a team project and let your co-worker take the credit for it at the end. Response 2 is an acceptable response. Making your leader/manager aware of the problem at an early stage will allow them to give the correct credit to the most deserving. Response 3 is the most effective response. Addressing the situation with your co-worker might make him step up his game and participate in the project before further action is required. Response 4 would be irresponsible. You should not let other people's lack of participation make you quit, this will reflect badly on you as an individual and a team member. Perseverance is key!

Q9. 1 = A, 2 = C, 3 = C, 4 = B

EXPLANATION = Response 1 would be the most appropriate. Talking to your manager and implementing a presentation strategy may convince other employees that your idea is a good one. Response 2 would be ineffective. Not taking any further action because people don't agree with it shows inability to work through criticism. You are a team leader, and were chosen for a reason, so you need to discuss your ideas, however good or bad they may be. Response 3 would also be irresponsible. Putting it into action without discussing it further could jeopardise your position and more so, the company. Response 4 is an acceptable response. Trying to influence employees shows your will power and determination to see an idea through.

Q10. 1 = C, 2 = B, 3 = C, 4 = A

EXPLANATION = Response 1 and 3 are ineffective responses. Allowing the employee to continuously turn up late, despite him making up the time, shows that you are 'soft' on disciplinary action. It is unfair for other employees if that person is allowed to turn up late. Making exceptions for one person is not effective because it will cause conflict for other employees. Response 2 is an acceptable response, but given the employee's habits, he is unlikely to change his time keeping skills on the basis of being on 'one last chance'. Issuing a formal warning is the most appropriate response. It demonstrates disciplinary action when required and provides a reasonable action to take.

Q11. 1 = C, 2 = A, 3 = C, 4 = B

EXPLANATION = Response 1 would be least effective. Leaving your shift without any cover will jeopardise your position in the company. It shows a lack of respect for the job and unprofessionalism. Response 2 would be the most appropriate, phoning your partner to say you are running late, will allow you to cover until your colleague arrives. Response 3 is also unacceptable. Telling a colleague information that needs to be passed on to the next person on shift may not get to her, the information may get lost in translation. Response 4 is an acceptable response. Letting your colleague know when they arrive that you had made plans but had to cover for her instead, shows that you were courteous enough to stay, but it affected your arranged plans for the evening.

Q12. 1 = B, 2 = B, 3 = C, 4 = C

EXPLANATION = Response 1 is an acceptable response. Asking your colleagues if they feel the same way you do in regards to political views being enforced in your work, could help you state a case if you take further action.

Response 2 is also an acceptable response. Letting your manager know your concerns could help the situation and resolve the problem. Responses 3 and 4 demonstrates a lack of professionalism. Both these responses could jeopardise your career in the Civil Service.

Q13. 1 = B, 2 = C, 3 = C, 4 = B

EXPLANATION = Response 1 is an acceptable response. As a supervisor you should be able to offer advice and support to employees in order to make them feel more competent and confident in their roles. Response 2 is unacceptable. You are the supervisor so should be dealing with such situations; going to the manager for something like this seems somewhat ineffective. Response 3 is also unacceptable. Not helping the employee will not help improve his performance in his role. Response 4 is an acceptable response. He is still on a probationary period, the job needs to satisfy the person and if they are not happy, they could consider other options.

Q14. 1 = C, 2 = C, 3 = A, 4 = B

EXPLANATION = Response 1 would be unacceptable. Ignoring the problem, particularly if he is ignoring instructions, will cause a problem in the efficiency of the workforce and possibly compromise the job in hand. Response 2 is also unacceptable. Raising your voice and using hostile and aggressive language is unprofessional and is likely to cause a bigger problem than actually resolving it. Response 3 is the most appropriate. Before doing anything, you should reflect what to do in the staff handbook you were given. This will give you an understanding of how to proceed. Response 4 is an acceptable response. Raising the issue with a member of management will quickly resolve the problem, however reading the handbook first will give you clearer instruction as to how to correctly deal with the situation.

Q15. 1 = C, 2 = C, 3 = B, 4 = A

EXPLANATION = Response 1 and 2 are unacceptable. It would be unacceptable to be late for an important meeting and will show a lack of professionalism. It would also be unprofessional to cancel the meeting one hour before it commences. Response 3 is acceptable. Odds are you would have memorised important information and would have some idea of what you were going to say. Response 4 would be most appropriate. One hour gives you enough time to write down everything you remember from your previous work and quickly make some new notes, so you are prepared to go into the meeting with a clearer indication of what to talk about.

Q16. 1 = B, 2 = C, 3 = A, 4 = C

EXPLANATION = Response 1 is an acceptable response. Telling a co-worker will ensure that the manager receives an explanation as to your whereabouts. Response 2 is unacceptable. You cannot assume that you might not get caught and therefore would be acceptable to leave without telling anyone; it would not be acceptable and demonstrates a lack of professionalism. Response 3 is the most appropriate. Calling your manager and letting them know directly will ensure that the correct information is given and that they are fully briefed about your personal problems. Response 4 is unacceptable. Waiting until after you get back to let someone know where you have been is unprofessional and ineffective.

Q17. 1 = B, 2 = C, 3 = C, 4 = A

EXPLANATION = Response 1 is an acceptable response. Letting management know your concerns will allow the problem to be dealt with in the most professional and correct way. Response 2 and 3 are unacceptable. Speaking to other colleagues or raising the issue publically might make matters worse, not to mention it will humiliate your co-worker. Response 4 is the most appropriate response. Talking to your co-worker and offering support offers reassurance and help which may help the co-worker confess to anything that may be struggling for him.

Q18. 1 = C, 2 = A, 3 = C, 4 = C

EXPLANATION = Responses 1, 3 and 4 are all unacceptable. You cannot blame it on someone else, nor can you leave it till the very last minute to tell your manager or not saying anything at all. All three are irresponsible and unprofessional. Response 2 is the most appropriate. It is important that you are able to own up to your mistakes and inform your manager immediately of that mistake.

Q19. 1 = B, 2 = A, 3 = C, 4 = C

EXPLANATION = Response 1 is an acceptable response. Reiterating the protocol and expectations as employees will not only address the current situation, but reinforce what is expected from everyone. Response 2 is the most appropriate. Addressing the two colleagues who are causing a cause for concern need to be addressed directly and firmly to ensure they understand what is expected. Responses 3 and 4 are unacceptable. Ignoring the problem is not going to resolve anything, nor is asking someone to monitor the two colleagues – they are adults, they shouldn't have to be treated like children.

Q20. 1 = C, 2 = C, 3 = A, 4 = C

EXPLANATION = Responses 1, 2 and 4 are all unacceptable. Creating an argument will not help the matter. Going to management and asking them to demand the phone back is impractical. You have no evidence to suggest that the phone is actually yours. It would also be impractical to snoop through someone else's possessions, it will just cause more trouble for yourself. Response 3 is the most appropriate. Checking the CCTV will validate whether it is your phone or not and then action can be made if necessary.

Q21. 1 = C, 2 = B, 3 = A, 4 = C

EXPLANATION = Responses 1 and 4 are unacceptable. You should let someone know if you are feeling unwell. You should make sure they are aware of your illness in case you need to go home. You should not leave work without saying anything to anyone. Response 2 is acceptable. You should inform your supervisor if you are unwell, so they are aware. Response 4 is most appropriate because it gives them notice as to what is wrong and why you may not be in work the next day.

Q22. 1 = C, 2 = C, 3 = A, 4 = C

EXPLANATION = Responses 1, 2 and 4 are unacceptable because it shows unprofessionalism and immaturity. Response 3 shows your ability to persevere and carry on with the work that you should be doing without little fuss.

Q23. 1 = C, 2 = B, 3 = B, 4 = B

EXPLANATION = Response 1 is unacceptable. It is not your place to give a warning to another colleague, they probably wouldn't listen to you anyway, so taking the situation into your own hands is impractical. Responses 2, 3 and 4 are all acceptable. You would be addressing the harassment issue in some way by acting on it professionally.

Q24. 1 = C, 2 = A, 3 = C, 4 = C

EXPLANATION = Responses 1, 3 and 4 are unacceptable. They all lack professionalism and would not resolve the situation. Response 2 will politely and professionally deal with the incident in a correct and proficient manner without causing any controversy.

Q25. 1 = C, 2 = A, 3 = C, 4 = B

EXPLANATION = Responses 1 and 3 are unacceptable. You should not accept the tickets as well, nor should you play ignorant and ignore the situation. Response 2 is the most appropriate. You should refuse the tickets and recommend to your colleague that they should return the gift. It is the most professional and correct thing to do. Response 4 is an acceptable response, informing higher authorities will make sure the incident gets dealt with in a proficient manner.

Q26. 1 = C, 2 = B, 3 = C, 4 = A

EXPLANATION = Responses 1 and 3 are unacceptable. You shouldn't feel the need to help with his workload, everyone has a tough workload and they need to deal with it efficiently. Asking for an extension is unprofessional. Response 2 allows you to inform your supervisor of your concerns which may help the situation. Response 4 is the most appropriate. Directly talking to your colleague about your concerns and reiterating the strict deadline may make your colleague work more efficiently.

Q27. 1 = C, 2 = B, 3 = C, 4 = A

EXPLANATION = Response 1 would be unacceptable. You don't want to make the meeting a competition of who can be heard and authoritative the most. Response 2 is acceptable. Talking to your supervisor prior to the next meeting will implement a new strategy. Response 3 is unacceptable. You should not refuse the opportunity of representing the company after you have already agreed to it just because you are unable to work effectively with somebody. Response 4 is the most appropriate. Explaining to your supervisor your concerns and feelings in relation to the meetings is the most professional way of dealing with the problem.

Q28. 1 = B, 2 = B, 3 = B, 4 = C

EXPLANATION = Responses 1, 2 and 3 are all acceptable and reasonable. You could just admit to the rumours, you have nothing to hide. Waiting until you know for sure is also reasonable because there is no point making a point out of nothing. Telling your employer's seems a courteous thing to do. Response 4 is unacceptable because lying to your employees shows lack of respect, and could compromise your position if you decide to stay.

Q29. 1 = C, 2 = C, 3 = A, 4 = B

EXPLANATION = Responses 1 and 2 are unacceptable. You cannot just not turn up to work without informing anyone. Neither is it a good idea to take your child to work without someone agreeing to it, and hoping that you don't get caught, it is not professional. Response 3 is the most appropriate. Phoning your supervisor prior to starting work will allow your supervisor to decide what to do. Response 4 is an acceptable response providing you arrive before you start work and not when you are supposed to start.

Q30. 1 = B, 2 = B, 3 = B, 4 = B

EXPLANATION = all four responses are reasonable and acceptable responses to make. They all are valid points of action you could take in regards to choosing whether to apply for the promotion or not.

Q31. 1 = C, 2 = A, 3 = C, 4 = C

EXPLANATION = Responses 1, 3 and 4 are unacceptable. You should not defer a person to apply for a job because your friend is applying for it. Nor should you rudely tell that person that they are not cut out for it. Telling him to apply for the job even though you know it will affect his confidence is unprofessional, you should be supportive as opposed to ridiculing employees. Response 2 is the most appropriate. It allows you to tell that person what you personally believe, and guide him in his decision.

Q32. 1 = C, 2 = A, 3 = C, 4 = C

EXPLANATION = Responses 1, 3 and 4 are all unacceptable. Responses 1 and 3 indicate that you may have a problem with her working because of her health condition. Response 4 suggests that there would be no change or accommodating factors put into place because she has a health condition, her health must be accommodated for. Response 2 is the most appropriate, letting her know amendments can be made to make her job easier demonstrates your acceptance of different types of employee's needs.

Q33. 1 = A, 2 = C, 3 = C, 4 = C

EXPLANATION = Response 1 is the most appropriate. It gives you a plan of how to move forward and make sure the work gets done on time. Responses 2, 3 and 4 are unacceptable. You cannot make the other two members of the team work more just to accommodate their inability to stick to deadlines. Nor should you go to the managing director to ask for an extension. It shows lack of commitment and the inability to stick to deadlines and work effectively as a team.

Q34. 1 = C, 2 = A, 3 = B, 4 = C

EXPLANATION = Responses 1 and 4 are unacceptable. You need to encourage the shy employee to participate more rather than make him feel more apprehensive. Response 2 is the most appropriate. It is a direct and professional way to encourage him to take part without belittling him. Response

3 is an acceptable response. Trying to encourage and support him subtly might give him more courage to actively participate. This way he won't feel as though he has been judged.

Q35. 1 = C, 2 = A, 3 = C, 4 = B

EXPLANATION = Responses 1 and 3 are unacceptable. Research on the internet is not going to give you an insight into the way their department is going to run, you are only going to find out general facts, which probably won't help in the long run. It would be irresponsible not to do anything before you start your job. Response 2 is the most appropriate. It shows your professionalism and ability to handle a stressful situation and dealing with it in the most appropriate manner. Response 4 is an acceptable response, asking for any information by email is probably more convenient to the senior manager and therefore will be more willing to give you some advice.

Q36. 1 = A, 2 = C, 3 = B, 4 = C

EXPLANATION = Response 1 is the most appropriate. Having regular meetings with all team members will ensure that everyone knows what they are doing, problems and issues can be dealt with accordingly and everyone will feel more confident in their job. Responses 2 and 4 are unacceptable. Ignoring the problem could make things worse, it would be irresponsible to hope things will improve. It is also unacceptable to inform your team member of their careless work but not give them any advice or support. Response 3 is acceptable. Directly giving objectives and goals to each team member will ensure that they know what their task is, and gives them the chance to state any problems that they might be having.

Q37. 1 = C, 2 = A, 3 = B, 4 = C

EXPLANATION = Responses 1 and 4 are unacceptable. If you are feeling overwhelmed then the issue should not be ignored and should be resolved quickly in order to make sure your work is efficient. Response 2 is the most appropriate. Making action plans and scheduling your workload will relieve the pressure and make you feel more confident. Response 4 is an acceptable response. Speaking with someone higher than yourself will ensure you are given informative advice and information in regards to managing your job role.

Q38. 1 = C, 2 = C, 3 = B, 4 = A

EXPLANATION = Responses 1 and 2 are unacceptable. The issue should not be brought to everyone's attention, and should be dealt with in a more covert and professional manner. Response 3 is an acceptable response. Directly speaking with the employee might resolve the issue, or at least gain more clarity and understanding about how to deal with it from there. Response 4 is the most appropriate. Letting higher authorities deal with the problem will ensure the problem gets managed in a professional and authoritative way.

Q39. 1 = C, 2 = C, 3 = B, 4 = B

EXPLANATION = Responses 1 and 2 are both unacceptable. You should not hope that you will be back in time and go without telling anyone. Nor should you go to your appointment and not return to work after. Response 3 and 4 are acceptable. It demonstrates a professional way of dealing with such situations and ensures that your supervisor knows where you are and the reason you may be late.

Q40. 1 = C, 2 = A, 3 = C, 4 = C

EXPLANATION = Responses 1, 3 and 4 are unacceptable. You still have time to finish the project off and submit it by the end of the day. Telling a co-worker does not solve the problem, nor does worrying about it later when it would be too late. Response 2 is the most appropriate and the most professional. Quickly finishing the project and then joining the party gives you the best of both worlds – knowing your work is completely finished and being able to enjoy the Christmas party without worrying about the project.

Remember, we have also provided you with some additional free online psychometric tests which will help to further improve your competence in this particular testing area. To gain access, simply go to:

www.PsychometricTestsOnline.co.uk

Good luck with your Civil Service Qualifying (Non-Fast Stream) Tests. We wish you the best of luck with all your future endeavours!

The How2become team

Get more books, manuals, online tests and training courses at:

www.How2Become.com

Printed in Great Britain
by Amazon